BEGINNER'S G
MENTAL EXERCISES
FOR DOGS

A step-by-step guide to establish a strong bond and keep the dog engaged and happy

BONUS #1

Daily mental stimulation planner

BONUS #2

Tracking progress and behavioral changes worksheet

BONUS #3

Checklist of essential supplies for mental exercises

Kathy Reynold

Table of Contents

INTRODUCTION

TO CANINE

MENTAL STIMULATION

Chapter 1:

The Importance of Mental Exercises for Dogs

THE BENEFITS OF MENTAL STIMULATION

Mental stimulation is an indispensable aspect of a dog's overall well-being and happiness. Just like humans, dogs require mental exercise to keep their minds sharp and engaged. Providing your furry friend with adequate mental stimulation offers a range of benefits, ensuring they lead a balanced and fulfilled life. Listed below are the various advantages of mental stimulation for dogs, helping you understand why it is crucial for their overall health and happiness.

➤ **Prevents Boredom**

Dogs are intelligent creatures that thrive on mental challenges. When left without mental stimulation, they can quickly become bored and restless. Boredom often leads to undesirable behaviors such as excessive barking, chewing on furniture, digging, or even aggression. By providing your dog with stimulating activities, you can keep them mentally occupied.

➤ **Reduces Anxiety and Stress**

Mental stimulation has a calming effect on dogs, helping to reduce anxiety and stress. Engaging their minds in various activities helps redirect their focus and energy away from negative emotions. Puzzles, interactive toys, and training exercises are excellent ways to stimulate their brains and promote relaxation.

➤ Enhances Problem-Solving Skills

Mental stimulation encourages dogs to think and problem-solve. Engaging them in activities that require decision-making and critical thinking helps sharpen their cognitive abilities. By presenting them with different challenges, you allow them to exercise their problem-solving skills and boost their intelligence.

➤ Builds Confidence

Dogs that receive regular mental stimulation often exhibit increased confidence and self-assurance. As they conquer various challenges and learn new skills, they develop a sense of accomplishment and pride. This, in turn, translates into a more confident demeanor in their everyday lives.

➤ Fosters Bonding and Communication

Engaging in mentally stimulating activities with your dog strengthens the bond between you and your furry companion. Training sessions, interactive play, and problem-solving tasks create opportunities for positive interactions and communication. Through these shared experiences, you establish a deeper connection and understanding with your dog.

➤ Reduces Destructive Behavior

Dogs with pent-up energy and lack of mental stimulation are more likely to engage in destructive behavior. Engaging dogs in mentally stimulating activities helps redirect their energy towards positive outlets, ultimately reducing the likelihood of destructive behaviors.

➤ Increases Focus and Attention

Mental stimulation exercises a dog's ability to concentrate and focus on specific tasks. This enhanced focus and attention span can have practical applications in various aspects of their lives, such as obedience training or participating in dog sports. By regularly engaging their minds, you improve their ability to stay attentive and responsive to your commands.

➤ **Alleviates Boredom-Related Eating Disorders**

Dogs that are bored or lack mental stimulation are more prone to developing eating disorders, such as overeating or compulsive eating. By providing them with mental exercises, you offer a healthy outlet for their energy and reduce the likelihood of them resorting to unhealthy eating habits.

➤ **Slows Cognitive Decline in Senior Dogs**

Mental stimulation is particularly crucial for senior dogs. Just like humans, older dogs can experience cognitive decline as they age. Engaging their minds through interactive games and gentle training exercises can help slow down this decline and keep their cognitive abilities sharp.

➤ **Provides Physical Exercise**

While mental stimulation primarily focuses on exercising a dog's mind, many mentally stimulating activities also provide physical exercise. Activities such as agility training, scent work, or interactive play require physical exertion, contributing to a well-rounded exercise routine. This helps maintain a healthy weight, promotes cardiovascular health, and enhances overall physical fitness.

UNDERSTANDING YOUR DOG'S COGNITIVE NEEDS

Dogs are intelligent creatures with complex minds, and catering to their cognitive requirements is just as important as meeting their physical needs. By recognizing and addressing their cognitive needs, you can ensure that your furry companion remains mentally stimulated and engaged, leading to improved overall well-being.

One crucial aspect of understanding your dog's cognitive needs is recognizing their intelligence and problem-solving abilities. Dogs possess varying levels of intelligence, and it's important to tailor mental stimulation activities to their specific cognitive abilities. Some dogs may excel at complex tasks and puzzles, while others may require simpler challenges. By observing your dog's behavior and assessing their problem-solving skills, you can provide appropriate cognitive exercises that match their abilities, ensuring they are neither overwhelmed nor bored.

Another aspect of understanding your dog's cognitive needs is acknowledging their need for novelty and variety. Dogs, like humans, can become bored with repetitive routines. Introducing new toys, games, and activities keeps their minds engaged and prevents monotony. Rotate toys regularly, offer different types of puzzles, and incorporate a variety of training exercises to provide a stimulating environment that constantly presents new challenges. This not only prevents boredom but also encourages curiosity and exploration, which are vital for cognitive development.

Additionally, recognizing the importance of social interaction and communication is crucial for meeting your dog's cognitive needs. Dogs are social animals that thrive on human interaction and companionship. Engaging in activities that involve training, play, and bonding time strengthens the bond between you and your dog while stimulating their cognitive abilities. Training sessions, obedience classes, and interactive play not only provide mental stimulation but also foster communication skills and promote positive behavioral patterns.

Furthermore, understanding your dog's cognitive needs involves being aware of their individual preferences and interests. Just like humans, dogs have unique personalities and inclinations. Some dogs may be more inclined towards problem-solving puzzles, while others may enjoy scent work or agility training. By identifying their preferences and tailoring mental stimulation activities accordingly, you can ensure that your dog remains engaged and motivated. Pay attention to what activities they find most stimulating and rewarding, and incorporate those into their routine.

It is also important to acknowledge that cognitive needs change as dogs age. Puppies have a greater need for exploration, play, and learning, while senior dogs may require gentle mental exercises that support cognitive function and memory. Adapting mental stimulation activities to suit their age and capabilities helps maintain cognitive health and prevents cognitive decline in senior dogs.

HOW MENTAL EXERCISES CONTRIBUTE TO OVERALL WELL-BEING

While physical exercise is crucial for maintaining a healthy body, mental stimulation is equally important for a balanced and fulfilling life. Engaging in mental exercises provides numerous benefits that enhance cognitive abilities, emotional stability, and overall quality of life. Let's explore how mental exercises contribute to the overall well-being of individuals.

➢ **Cognitive Health**

Mental exercises stimulate the brain, improving cognitive function and promoting brain health. Regular mental stimulation helps maintain cognitive abilities, including memory, attention, problem-solving, and decision-making skills. By challenging the brain through various activities or engaging in intellectual discussions, individuals can keep their minds sharp and reduce the risk of cognitive decline.

➢ **Emotional Well-being**

Mental exercises have a positive impact on emotional well-being. Engaging in activities that challenge the mind promotes the release of endorphins, the "feel-good" hormones that elevate mood and reduce stress and anxiety. Mental stimulation also encourages individuals to focus their attention on the present moment, fostering mindfulness and reducing negative thought patterns. This, in turn, enhances emotional stability and resilience.

➢ **Stress Reduction**

Mental exercises serve as a powerful tool for stress reduction. When the mind is occupied with challenging and engaging activities, individuals are less likely to dwell on stressors or ruminate on negative thoughts. Mental stimulation distracts from daily worries, allowing individuals to shift their focus and attain a state of relaxation. Activities such as meditation, problem-solving, or engaging in creative pursuits can significantly reduce stress levels and promote a sense of calm.

➢ **Increased Creativity**

Mental exercises stimulate creativity and innovative thinking. By engaging in activities that require problem-solving, brainstorming, or exploring new ideas, individuals can expand their creative potential. Mental stimulation encourages the brain to think outside the box, make new connections, and generate innovative solutions. This creative boost contributes to a sense of fulfillment and self-expression, leading to a more satisfying and enriching life.

➢ **Enhanced Learning Abilities**

Regular mental exercises improve learning abilities and the capacity to acquire new knowledge and skills. When the brain is consistently challenged, it becomes more adept at absorbing and retaining information. Mental stimulation promotes neural plasticity, allowing the brain to form new connections and strengthen existing ones. This heightened learning capacity opens doors to personal growth, career development, and a broader understanding of the world.

➢ **Social Engagement**

Mental exercises often involve social interaction, which contributes to overall well-being. Engaging in group activities, discussions, or team-based mental challenges fosters social connections and a sense of belonging. Collaboration with others in problem-solving activities promotes teamwork, communication skills, and cooperation. The social aspect of mental exercises enriches interpersonal relationships and creates a supportive network, which is essential for mental and emotional health.

➢ **Lifelong Learning and Personal Development**

Mental exercises encourage lifelong learning and personal development. They promote curiosity, a thirst for knowledge, and a continuous desire to grow and expand one's abilities. Engaging in mental challenges and acquiring new skills or knowledge keeps individuals intellectually stimulated and motivated. This pursuit of personal growth enhances self-esteem, self-confidence, and a sense of purpose.

PART 1

GETTING STARTED WITH MENTAL EXERCISES

Chapter 1:

Building a Strong Foundation

ESTABLISHING TRUST AND COMMUNICATION

Trust forms the cornerstone of any strong relationship, and this is especially true when it comes to your bond with your dog. Building trust involves consistency, positive reinforcement, and understanding. Here are some key ways to establish trust with your dog:

✓ Consistency: Dogs thrive on routine and predictability. Establish consistent rules, boundaries, and routines to help your dog feel secure and understand what is expected of them. Consistency also applies to your interactions and responses. By being consistent in your commands and expectations, you build trust with your dog.

✓ Positive Reinforcement: Positive reinforcement is a powerful tool for building trust and reinforcing desired behaviors. Reward your dog with treats, praise, and affection when they exhibit good behavior or successfully complete a task. This positive reinforcement strengthens the bond between you and your dog and encourages them to repeat the behavior.

✓ Clear Communication: Effective communication is crucial for building trust and understanding between you and your dog. Use clear and concise verbal cues and hand signals to communicate commands. Be mindful of your body language and tone of voice, as dogs are highly attuned to non-verbal cues. Consistent and clear communication helps your dog comprehend what is expected of them and builds trust in your guidance.

BASIC TRAINING TECHNIQUES FOR MENTAL STIMULATION

Basic training not only teaches your dog important skills but also provides mental stimulation and challenges their cognitive abilities. Here are some training techniques that promote mental stimulation:

✓ Sit, Stay, and Down: Teaching your dog basic obedience commands such as sit, stay, and down not only ensures their safety but also engages their minds. Start with short training sessions, using positive reinforcement to reward desired behaviors. As your dog becomes more proficient, gradually increase the difficulty level, introducing distractions or longer durations for stays.

✓ Recall Training: Recall training is vital for keeping your dog safe and promoting mental stimulation. Begin in a low-distraction environment and use a recall command, such as "come," paired with positive reinforcement when your dog responds. Gradually increase the difficulty level by practicing in more distracting environments or using longer distances.

✓ Trick Training: Teaching your dog tricks is a fun way to stimulate their minds and build a stronger bond. Tricks like "shake paw," "roll over," or "play dead" require problem-solving and memory skills. Break down each trick into small steps, using positive reinforcement and repetition. With consistency and patience, your dog will master these tricks and enjoy the mental challenge they provide.

✓ Interactive Toys and Puzzle Games: Incorporate interactive toys and puzzle games into your dog's routine. These toys engage their problem-solving skills and keep them mentally stimulated. Puzzle toys with hidden treats or compartments that require manipulation and problem-solving are particularly beneficial. Rotate toys regularly to maintain novelty and prevent boredom.

INCORPORATING MENTAL EXERCISES INTO DAILY LIFE

Mental exercises shouldn't be limited to specific training sessions or playtime. Integrating mental stimulation into your dog's daily life helps keep their minds actively engaged. Here are some ways to incorporate mental exercises into your dog's routine:

➢ **Daily Walks**

A daily walk is an excellent opportunity for mental stimulation. Allow your dog to explore new environments, encounter different scents, and encounter mild challenges such as walking over different surfaces or navigating obstacles. Encourage sniffing and investigating their surroundings, as it provides mental stimulation and engages their senses.

➢ **Food Dispensing Toys**

Instead of feeding your dog from a traditional bowl, use food-dispensing toys or puzzle feeders. These toys require your dog to figure out how to access their food, providing mental stimulation while satisfying their hunger. It also helps slow down their eating, promoting healthier digestion.

➢ **Nose Work**

Dogs have an incredible sense of smell, and engaging their noses in nose work activities is mentally stimulating. Hide treats or toys around the house or in the yard, and encourage your dog to use their sense of smell to find them. You can also consider enrolling in formal scent work classes or competitions, where your dog can use their scenting abilities in a structured and challenging setting.

➢ **Training During Daily Activities**

Incorporate training into everyday activities, such as mealtime or going through doorways. Ask your dog to sit or wait before you place their food bowl down or before opening the door. These small training exercises reinforce good behavior and provide mental stimulation in routine situations.

➢ **Play and Engage**

Playtime is not just for physical exercise but can also be mentally stimulating. Incorporate interactive games like hide-and-seek or fetch, which require problem-solving and mental engagement. Regularly switch out their toys to introduce new and exciting options.

Remember, every dog is unique, and it's important to tailor mental exercises to their individual needs, abilities, and preferences. Observe your dog's reactions and adjust the level of difficulty or the type of mental exercise accordingly. Building a strong foundation with your dog through trust, communication, basic training, and mental stimulation not only strengthens your bond but also promotes their overall well-being and leads to a happier, more fulfilled life.

Chapter 2:

Understanding Canine Intelligence

DIFFERENT TYPES OF CANINE INTELLIGENCE

Canine intelligence is a fascinating subject, and dogs exhibit various types of intelligence that contribute to their problem-solving abilities, learning capacity, and overall cognitive skills. While it's important to note that intelligence can vary among individual dogs, researchers have identified different types of canine intelligence based on their specific strengths and abilities.

➢ **Instinctive Intelligence**

Instinctive intelligence refers to a dog's natural abilities and instincts that are inherited from their breed or ancestral lineage. Different breeds have been selectively bred for specific purposes, such as herding, hunting, guarding, or retrieving. Dogs with high instinctive intelligence excel in tasks related to their breed's original purpose. For example, herding breeds like Border Collies have a strong instinct for herding and exhibit exceptional problem-solving skills when it comes to controlling and guiding livestock.

➢ **Adaptive Intelligence**

Adaptive intelligence refers to a dog's ability to learn from and adapt to new situations or environments. Dogs with high adaptive intelligence can quickly understand and adjust their behavior to changing circumstances. They possess excellent problem-solving skills and can apply their past experiences to novel situations. This type of intelligence is often observed in working and service dog breeds, as they need to adapt to various tasks and environments to fulfill their roles effectively.

➤ **Obedience Intelligence**

Obedience intelligence refers to a dog's ability to understand and follow commands or cues from their human handlers. Dogs with high obedience intelligence are quick to learn and exhibit a strong desire to please their owners. They are attentive, responsive, and can master a wide range of commands and tasks. Breeds like Border Collies, German Shepherds, and Golden Retrievers often excel in obedience training and can perform complex tasks with precision and reliability.

➤ **Problem-Solving Intelligence**

Problem-solving intelligence refers to a dog's ability to analyze and solve problems. Dogs with high problem-solving intelligence exhibit advanced cognitive skills and can figure out solutions to challenges or puzzles. They demonstrate excellent observational skills, logical thinking, and the ability to overcome obstacles. This type of intelligence is often observed in breeds like Poodles, Australian Shepherds, and Rottweilers, who excel in activities that require problem-solving, such as agility courses or interactive puzzle toys.

➤ **Social Intelligence**

Social intelligence refers to a dog's ability to understand and interact effectively with other animals, including humans and fellow dogs. Dogs with high social intelligence demonstrate excellent communication skills, empathy, and the ability to read social cues. They can understand human emotions and respond accordingly. Breeds like Labrador Retrievers, Cavalier King Charles Spaniels, and Boxers are known for their high social intelligence, making them great therapy or assistance dogs.

➤ **Sensory Intelligence**

Sensory intelligence refers to a dog's heightened senses and their ability to interpret and respond to sensory information. Dogs have a superior sense of smell, hearing, and vision compared to humans, and breeds that excel in sensory intelligence have a heightened sensitivity to their environment. For instance, Bloodhounds have an exceptional sense of smell and are often used in tracking and search operations due to their ability to detect and follow scents. Sight hounds like Greyhounds have remarkable visual acuity and speed, allowing them to excel in activities like lure coursing.

It's important to recognize that these different types of intelligence are not mutually exclusive, and many dogs exhibit a combination of these qualities. Additionally, individual dogs within a breed may vary in their strengths and aptitudes.

ASSESSING YOUR DOG'S STRENGTHS AND WEAKNESSES

Understanding your dog's unique abilities, preferences, and areas that may need improvement is a crucial part of assessing their strengths and weaknesses. This knowledge enables you to tailor your approach to their training and provide the necessary support. By identifying their strengths, you can capitalize on their talents and provide suitable outlets for them to thrive. Conversely, recognizing weaknesses allows you to address them through targeted training and offer additional assistance as required. In this section, we will delve into the process of assessing your dog's strengths and weaknesses and explore how you can utilize this understanding to enhance their overall well-being.

➢ **Observation and Interaction**

The first step in assessing your dog's strengths and weaknesses is to spend quality time observing and interacting with them. Observe their behavior, reactions, and responses in various situations and environments. Note their preferred activities, interactions with other dogs or humans, and any particular behaviors or skills that stand out.

Pay attention to the following areas:

✓ Physical Abilities: Observe your dog's physical capabilities, such as speed, agility, endurance, and coordination. Note if they excel in activities that require physical strength or have any limitations or difficulties in specific movements.

✓ Temperament and Personality: Assess your dog's temperament and personality traits. Are they outgoing and confident or more reserved and cautious? Do they adapt well to new situations, or do they tend to be anxious or fearful? Understanding their temperament helps determine the best approach to training and socialization.

- ✓ Communication Skills: Observe how well your dog communicates with you and other dogs or animals. Do they understand and respond to verbal commands or body language cues? Are they good at expressing their needs or emotions? Communication skills play a crucial role in training and overall well-being.

- ✓ Social Interactions: Assess how your dog interacts with other dogs, animals, and humans. Do they enjoy socializing and playing with other dogs? Are they comfortable around new people or do they display signs of fear or aggression? Understanding their social interactions helps create a safe and positive environment for them.

➢ **Training and Skill Assessment**

Training and skill assessment involve evaluating your dog's abilities in specific areas and identifying areas that may require further training or improvement. This assessment can help you tailor training programs to focus on their strengths and work on any weaknesses. Consider the following factors:

- ✓ Obedience and Basic Commands: Assess how well your dog responds to basic commands such as sit, stay, come, and heel. Determine their level of obedience and their understanding of commands. This assessment will help you gauge their level of training and identify areas that may need reinforcement.

- ✓ Specific Skills: Evaluate your dog's skills in activities specific to their breed or desired activities. For example, if you have a retriever, assess their retrieving skills and their ability to follow scent trails. If you have a herding breed, observe their herding instincts and their ability to respond to herding commands. This assessment will help you identify areas of natural talent and potential areas for further development.

- ✓ Problem-Solving Abilities: Assess your dog's problem-solving abilities by introducing them to puzzles or interactive toys. Observe how they approach challenges and if they can figure out solutions. This assessment can give you insight into their cognitive abilities and their capacity for problem-solving.

✓ Behavioral Issues: Identify any behavioral issues or challenges your dog may have, such as excessive barking, separation anxiety, or fear-based reactions. Understanding these issues helps you address them through training, behavior modification techniques, or seeking professional help if needed.

➢ **Seeking Professional Guidance**

In some cases, seeking professional guidance from a dog trainer, behaviorist, or veterinarian may be beneficial, especially when dealing with complex behavioral issues or specialized training requirements. A professional can provide an objective assessment of your dog's strengths and weaknesses and offer guidance on how to address specific areas of concern.

➢ **Working with Your Dog's Strengths and Weaknesses**

Once you have assessed your dog's strengths and weaknesses, you can create a plan to work with them effectively. Here are some strategies to consider:

✓ Capitalize on Strengths: Provide opportunities for your dog to engage in activities that align with their strengths. If they excel in physical activities, consider participating in agility or obedience trials. If they have strong problem-solving abilities, provide them with interactive toys or engage them in puzzle-solving games. By capitalizing on their strengths, you can provide outlets for their talents and keep them mentally and physically stimulated.

✓ Address Weaknesses through Training: For areas where your dog may have weaknesses, such as obedience or socialization, focus on targeted training. Break down tasks into small, manageable steps and use positive reinforcement techniques to encourage progress. Seek professional help if needed, especially when dealing with complex behavioral issues.

✓ Provide Mental Stimulation: Regardless of their strengths and weaknesses, all dogs benefit from mental stimulation. Incorporate activities that engage their minds, such as, scent work or obedience training sessions. Mental stimulation helps prevent a sense of monotony, strengthens their cognitive abilities, and contributes to their overall well-being.

✓ Practice Positive Reinforcement: Positive reinforcement is a powerful tool in training and building a strong bond with your dog. Reward their successes, no matter how small, with treats, praise, or playtime. Positive reinforcement encourages desired behaviors, boosts their confidence, and fosters a positive learning environment.

✓ Be Patient and Understanding: Every dog is unique, and progress may vary. Be patient with your dog as they learn and grow. Understand their limitations and provide a supportive and nurturing environment. Celebrate their successes and be understanding when they face challenges or setbacks.

Assessing your dog's strengths and weaknesses is an ongoing process. As they grow, learn, and experience new things, their abilities may change or develop further. Regularly reassess their skills, observe their behavior, and adapt your training and activities accordingly.

TAILORING EXERCISES TO STIMULATE SPECIFIC INTELLIGENCE AREAS

By identifying your dog's specific intelligence strengths and weaknesses, you can design activities that target and develop specific intelligence areas. Here, we provide examples of exercises to stimulate each intelligence area.

➢ **Instinctive Intelligence**

To stimulate instinctive intelligence, provide activities that tap into their breed's inherent skills. Here are some examples:

✓ Herding Breeds: Set up a mini-obstacle course using cones or other objects and guide your dog through it using commands such as "come by" or "away to me." You can also introduce them to herding balls or frisbees to encourage their herding instincts.

- ✓ Retrieving Breeds: Engage your dog in retrieving games, using toys or balls. Start with short distances and gradually increase the distance. Incorporate commands like "fetch" or "drop it" to enhance their retrieving skills.
- ✓ Scent Hounds: Hide treats or toys in your backyard or a designated area and encourage your dog to use their exceptional sense of smell to locate them. You can also introduce them to scent work activities, where they have to search for specific scents or objects.

➢ **Adaptive Intelligence**

To stimulate adaptive intelligence, provide activities that challenge their problem-solving abilities and encourage learning. Here are some examples:

- ✓ Puzzle Toys: Consider investing in toys that require your dog to figure out how to access treats or hidden compartments. Start with easier puzzles and gradually increase the difficulty level as your dog becomes more proficient.
- ✓ Hide and Seek: Hide treats or toys in different locations around your house or yard and encourage your dog to search for them. Increase the complexity by hiding them in more challenging spots or using scent cues to guide them.
- ✓ Training Variations: Vary your training routines and introduce new commands or tricks regularly. This keeps your dog engaged and encourages them to think and adapt to new tasks.

➢ **Obedience Intelligence**

To stimulate obedience intelligence, focus on training exercises that strengthen their responsiveness and reliability. Here are some examples:

- ✓ Basic Commands: Practice basic commands such as sit, stay, come, and heel in different environments and with increasing distractions. This helps your dog generalize the commands and respond reliably in various situations.

✓ Advanced Training: Teach your dog advanced commands or tricks like "roll over," "play dead," or "find it." These exercises challenge their obedience intelligence and enhance their learning capacity.

✓ Canine Sports: Engage your dog in activities like agility, rally obedience, or obedience competitions. These sports require precise obedience and help sharpen their responsiveness to commands.

➤ **Problem-Solving Intelligence**

To stimulate problem-solving intelligence, provide activities that require critical thinking and problem-solving skills. Here are some examples:

✓ Interactive Toys: Use toys that require your dog to solve puzzles to access treats or toys. These toys may have hidden compartments, sliding panels, or multiple layers that your dog needs to navigate.

✓ Treat Dispensing Games: Hide treats in a muffin tin covered with tennis balls. Your dog will have to remove the balls to access the treats. This exercise encourages them to use their problem-solving skills to get their rewards.

✓ Shape and Color Discrimination: Teach your dog to recognize and differentiate between shapes or colors. Start with simple exercises like matching toys to their corresponding shapes or colors and gradually increase the complexity.

➤ **Social Intelligence**

To stimulate social intelligence, engage your dog in activities that promote positive social interactions. Here are some examples:

✓ Playdates: Arrange playdates with other friendly and well-socialized dogs. This allows your dog to practice their social skills, including proper play behavior, sharing toys, and reading social cues from other dogs.

✓ Group Training Classes: Enroll your dog in group training classes where they can interact with other dogs and their owners under the guidance of a professional trainer. This provides a controlled and structured environment for socialization.

✓ Therapy Dog Programs: If your dog has a calm and friendly temperament, consider getting them certified as a therapy dog. This allows them to interact with different people in various settings, providing valuable socialization opportunities.

➤ **Sensory Intelligence**

To stimulate sensory intelligence, engage your dog in activities that focus on their senses. Here are some examples:

✓ Scent Work: Introduce your dog to scent work activities, where they have to search for specific scents or objects. Start with simple exercises and gradually increase the complexity and difficulty.

✓ Sound Recognition: Play different sounds, such as doorbells, sirens, or animal noises, and associate them with specific actions or commands. This helps your dog recognize and respond to different sounds.

✓ Visual Stimulation: Provide visual stimulation by showing your dog videos or movies featuring animals or nature scenes. This can captivate their attention and engage their visual senses.

PART 2

FUNDAMENTAL

MENTAL EXERCISES

Chapter 1:

Obedience Training for Mental Stimulation

BASIC COMMANDS AND THEIR ROLE IN MENTAL STIMULATION

Basic commands play a fundamental role in dog training and serve as the building blocks for more advanced obedience and mental stimulation. These commands establish a common language between you and your dog, promoting communication, discipline, and overall well-being. Let's explore the importance of basic commands in mental stimulation and how they contribute to your dog's cognitive development.

➤ Establishing Communication: Basic commands, such as sit, stay, come, and heel, provide a means of clear communication between you and your dog. When your dog understands and responds to these commands, it fosters a sense of trust, mutual understanding, and cooperation. This communication foundation is essential for further mental stimulation and advanced training.

➤ Promoting Focus and Attention: Teaching your dog basic commands requires their focus and attention. Through consistent training sessions, your dog learns to pay attention to your cues and respond accordingly. This focus and attention promote mental engagement, concentration, and the ability to follow instructions, which are all crucial aspects of mental stimulation.

➤ Enhancing Cognitive Skills: Learning and responding to basic commands stimulate your dog's cognitive skills. They have to process and understand verbal cues, associate them with specific actions, and execute the desired behavior. This mental processing enhances their ability to learn, problem-solve, and make connections between actions and consequences.

➢ Encouraging Self-Control: Basic commands promote self-control in dogs. When they learn to sit or stay on command, they develop the ability to resist impulses and exercise self-restraint. This self-control is valuable not only in training but also in various real-life situations, such as when encountering distractions or potentially dangerous scenarios.

Here's a step-by-step guide for teaching some of the basic commands:

Sit:
✓ Hold a treat close to your dog's nose, allowing them to smell it.
✓ Slowly raise the treat above their head, causing their nose to follow and their bottom to
✓ Once your dog is in a sitting position, say "sit" clearly and immediately reward them with the treat and praise.
✓ Repeat this process multiple times, gradually reducing the need to use the treat as a lure.

Stay:
✓ Ask your dog to sit or lie down.
✓ Hold your palm open in front of your dog's face and say "stay" in a firm but calm voice.
✓ Take a step back. If your dog stays in position, return to them, reward with praise, and a treat.
✓ Gradually increase the distance and duration of the stay, rewarding your dog each time they successfully maintain the stay command.
✓ Come:
✓ Begin in a secure and distraction-free environment.
✓ Crouch down, open your arms, and excitedly say "come" while patting your thighs.
✓ If your dog approaches you, reward them with praise and a treat.

✓ Practice the command in various locations, gradually introducing distractions and reinforcing the behavior with positive reinforcement.

Heel:

✓ Start with your dog on a leash and standing by your side.

✓ Begin walking and say "heel" in a clear voice.

✓ Hold the leash close to your body and keep your dog on your left side.

✓ Reward your dog for walking calmly by your side with praise, treats, or both.

✓ Practice walking in a straight line, stopping, and turning while maintaining the "heel" position.

PROGRESSING TO ADVANCED COMMANDS AND CHALLENGES

Once your dog has mastered the basic commands, it's important to progress to advanced commands and challenges to continue their mental stimulation and further their cognitive development. Advanced commands build upon the foundation established by the basics and provide additional mental challenges. Here's how you can progress to advanced commands and challenges:

➢ Adding Complexity to Basic Commands: Start by adding complexity and duration to the basic commands your dog already knows. For example, instead of asking them to sit for a few seconds, gradually increase the duration to a minute or more. Introduce distractions gradually to test their focus and self-control. This progression adds mental challenges and reinforces their understanding of the commands.

➢ Introducing New Commands: Once your dog has mastered the basics, introduce new commands to expand their repertoire. Advanced commands may include commands like "leave it," "take it," "spin," or "back up." These commands require additional cognitive processing and problem-solving skills from your dog.

Leave It:

✓ Hold a treat in your closed fist and present it to your dog.

✓ When your dog shows interest in the treat, say "leave it" in a firm but calm voice.

✓ Wait for your dog to lose interest in the treat and redirect their attention to you.

✓ Reward your dog with a different treat or praise when they disengage from the initial treat.

✓ Practice this command with different objects, gradually increasing the level of temptation.

Take It:

✓ Hold a toy or an object in your hand and show it to your dog.

✓ Say "take it" in an enthusiastic tone to encourage your dog to grab the object.

✓ When your dog makes an attempt to take the object, reward them with praise and playtime.

✓ Repeat this process, gradually increasing the distance between you and the object.

Spin:

✓ Start with your dog in a standing position in front of you.

✓ Hold a treat in front of your dog's nose and move it in a circular motion, leading your dog's head around in a circle.

✓ As your dog follows the treat with their head, say "spin" in a clear voice.

✓ Once your dog completes a full circle, reward them with the treat and praise.

✓ Repeat this process, gradually fading out the use of the treat as a lure.

Back Up:

✓ Stand facing your dog with a treat in your hand.

✓ Take a step towards your dog while saying "back up" in a firm tone.

✓ As your dog takes a step back, reward them with the treat and praise.

✓ Repeat this process, gradually increasing the distance your dog backs up.

➢ Incorporating Tricks and Complex Behaviors: Teach your dog tricks and complex behaviors that go beyond basic obedience. Tricks like rolling over, playing dead, or giving high fives provide mental stimulation and challenge their ability to learn and perform more intricate actions.

➤ Engaging in Canine Sports or Activities: Participating in canine sports, such as agility, rally obedience, or scent work, introduces new challenges and advanced commands. These sports require your dog to navigate obstacle courses, follow complex instructions, and demonstrate a high level of obedience and problem-solving ability.

USING POSITIVE REINFORCEMENT TECHNIQUES

Positive reinforcement techniques are crucial when training both basic and advanced commands. These techniques create a positive learning environment, foster trust and motivation, and enhance your dog's mental well-being. Here's how to effectively use positive reinforcement techniques:

➤ **Reward-Based Training**

Use rewards, such as treats, praise, or playtime, to reinforce your dog's correct response to commands. Immediately after they perform the desired behavior, offer a reward to associate the behavior with positive outcomes. This positive reinforcement strengthens the connection between the command and the desired action.

➤ **Timing and Consistency**

Be prompt and consistent in providing rewards. Timing is crucial as it helps your dog understand which behavior is being rewarded. Reward immediately after the correct response to ensure a clear association. Consistency in rewarding reinforces the behavior and promotes quicker learning.

➤ **Shaping Behavior**

Break down advanced commands or complex behaviors into smaller steps. Reward your dog for each small achievement towards the final goal. This shaping technique allows your dog to understand and progress gradually towards more complex behaviors, keeping them motivated and engaged.

➢ **Verbal and Physical Affection**

Alongside tangible rewards, use verbal praise and physical affection to reinforce your dog's positive behavior. Encouraging words, a gentle pat, or a belly rub can serve as powerful reinforcers and strengthen the bond between you and your dog.

➢ **Avoid Punishment**

Avoid using punishment-based techniques as they can hinder the learning process and cause fear or anxiety in your dog. Positive reinforcement focuses on rewarding desired behavior rather than punishing undesired behavior. This approach creates a positive and enjoyable training experience for your dog.

Chapter 2:

Interactive Play and Puzzle Toys

CHOOSING SUITABLE INTERACTIVE TOYS AND PUZZLES

When selecting interactive toys and puzzles for your dog, it's essential to consider their size, age, breed, and individual preferences. Here are some factors to keep in mind when choosing suitable interactive toys:

➢ Size and Durability: Choose toys that are appropriate for your dog's size and strength. Toys that are too small or fragile can pose a choking hazard or easily break, while toys that are too large may be difficult for smaller dogs to manipulate. Look for toys made from durable materials that can withstand your dog's play style.

➢ Complexity Level: Consider your dog's experience and skill level when selecting interactive toys and puzzles. Start with simpler toys and gradually increase the complexity as your dog becomes more proficient. Toys that offer adjustable difficulty levels are beneficial, as they can grow with your dog's abilities.

➢ Interactive Features: Look for toys that offer interactive features such as treat dispensing, hidden compartments, or moving parts. These features engage your dog's curiosity and encourage problem-solving behaviors. Toys that require your dog to manipulate or solve a puzzle to access a reward are particularly stimulating.

➢ Variety: Provide a variety of interactive toys to keep your dog engaged and prevent boredom. Rotate the toys regularly to maintain novelty and excitement. Offering different types of toys, such as plush toys, treat-dispensing toys, and puzzle toys, caters to your dog's diverse play and stimulation needs.

There are various interactive toys and puzzles available for dogs that can help keep them mentally stimulated and entertained. Here are some common types:

➢ Treat-Dispensing Toys: These toys have compartments or openings that can hold treats. Dogs have to figure out how to manipulate the toy to access the treats, keeping them engaged and rewarded.

➢ Puzzle Toys: Puzzle toys come in different shapes and designs. They usually have hidden compartments or movable parts that dogs need to manipulate to reveal treats or toys. These toys challenge your dog's problem-solving skills.

➢ Interactive Balls: Interactive balls are designed to keep dogs active and engaged. They may have treat compartments or make sounds to grab your dog's attention. Some interactive balls can even be controlled remotely, allowing you to play with your dog from a distance.

➢ Hide-and-Seek Toys: These toys involve hiding smaller toys or treats within a larger toy. Dogs have to use their sense of smell or solve simple puzzles to find the hidden items.

➢ Puzzle Mats and Snuffle Mats: Puzzle mats and snuffle mats are mats with various textures, flaps, and pockets. You can hide treats or kibble within the mat, and your dog has to search and use their nose to find them.

➢ Squeaky Toys: Squeaky toys engage dogs' curiosity and playfulness. Dogs learn to squeeze the toy to make a sound, providing a rewarding experience.

➢ Interactive Feeder Bowls: These are bowls designed with obstacles or patterns that slow down your dog's eating pace. By making mealtime more challenging, these bowls promote mental stimulation and help prevent rapid eating.

➢ Tug Toys: Tug toys are great for interactive play and bonding with your dog. They usually consist of a rope or a sturdy material that both you and your dog can grip, encouraging physical activity and mental engagement.

TEACHING PROBLEM-SOLVING SKILLS THROUGH PLAY

Dogs possess remarkable cognitive abilities and problem-solving skills, and developing these skills through play can have numerous benefits. Cognitive development is crucial for dogs, and engaging them in problem-solving activities can enhance their overall cognitive growth. Just like humans, dogs require mental stimulation to prevent boredom and associated behavioral issues. Problem-solving activities provide mental engagement and prevent cognitive decline.

Here are some exercises and games you can incorporate to teach problem-solving skills to your dog.

Treat-Seeking Game

This game helps dogs develop their problem-solving and scenting abilities.

Step-by-step guide:
- ✓ Start with a small number of treats and place them in plain sight while your dog watches.
- ✓ Encourage your dog to find and eat the treats.
- ✓ Gradually increase the difficulty by placing treats in hidden or slightly more challenging locations.
- ✓ Use verbal cues like "find it" or "search" to signal the start of the game.
- ✓ Over time, hide the treats in different rooms or outdoor areas to add more complexity.
- ✓ Eventually, you can progress to hiding treats in scent containers or puzzle toys to challenge your dog's scenting skills and problem-solving abilities.

Shell Game

This game involves cups or containers to hide treats and requires your dog to figure out which one holds the reward.

Step-by-step guide:
- ✓ Place three or more cups upside down on the floor in a row.

- ✓ Show your dog a treat and let them see you place it under one of the cups.
- ✓ Shuffle the cups quickly to mix them up.
- ✓ Encourage your dog to indicate the correct cup by touching it with their nose or paw.
- ✓ If they choose the correct cup, lift it to reveal the treat and praise your dog.
- ✓ If they choose the wrong cup, calmly show them that the treat was not there and allow them to try again.
- ✓ Gradually increase the difficulty by adding more cups or using faster shuffling motions.

Toy Puzzle

Using interactive puzzle toys challenges your dog's problem-solving skills while providing entertainment and mental stimulation.

Step-by-step guide:
- ✓ Select a puzzle toy that suits your dog's size, skill level, and preferences.
- ✓ Introduce the puzzle toy to your dog by showing them how it works.
- ✓ Place a few treats or pieces of kibble in the toy's compartments or hiding spots.
- ✓ Encourage your dog to manipulate the toy to access the treats.
- ✓ Offer verbal praise and encouragement as your dog successfully solves the puzzle.
- ✓ As your dog becomes more proficient, increase the complexity of the puzzle by adding more compartments or using different puzzle toys.
- ✓ Rotate and introduce new puzzle toys regularly to maintain your dog's interest and challenge their problem-solving skills.

DIY Obstacle Course

Setting up a DIY obstacle course encourages your dog to problem-solve and navigate through various challenges.

Step-by-step guide:
- ✓ Gather household items like cushions, boxes, tunnels, or cones to create obstacles.
- ✓ Arrange the obstacles in a safe and engaging manner in your indoor or outdoor space.

- ✓ Start with simple challenges, such as crawling under a low table or jumping over a small hurdle.
- ✓ Guide your dog through the course initially to familiarize them with the obstacles.
- ✓ Encourage your dog to navigate the course on their own, using verbal cues and hand signals as needed.
- ✓ Gradually increase the difficulty by adding more complex obstacles or rearranging the course layout.
- ✓ Reward your dog with treats and praise for successfully completing each obstacle or solving any challenges they encounter.

Muffin Tin Game

The muffin tin game is a simple yet effective problem-solving activity using everyday household items.

Step-by-step guide:
- ✓ Take a muffin tin and place some treats in a few of the cups.
- ✓ Cover each cup with tennis balls or other objects to hide the treats.
- ✓ Let your dog figure out how to remove the balls and find the treats.
- ✓ Encourage your dog to use their nose or paws to move the objects and reveal the treats.
- ✓ As your dog becomes more skilled, increase the difficulty by adding more cups or using different-sized objects to cover the treats.

Find the Hidden Toy

This game taps into your dog's natural instinct to search and find objects, encouraging problem-solving and scenting skills.

Step-by-step guide:
- ✓ Start by having your dog sit and stay in one area.
- ✓ Take a favorite toy and show it to your dog.
- ✓ While your dog is watching, hide the toy in an easily accessible location nearby.
- ✓ Release your dog from the stay command and say "Find it" or use a similar cue.

- ✓ Encourage your dog to search for the hidden toy using their nose and instincts.
- ✓ Once they find the toy, offer praise and reward them with playtime using the toy.
- ✓ Gradually increase the difficulty by hiding the toy in more challenging locations or in different rooms.

DIY Treat Dispenser

Creating your own treat dispenser adds a DIY element to the problem-solving activity and engages your dog's curiosity.

Step-by-step guide:
- ✓ Find a plastic bottle with a wide opening and remove the cap.
- ✓ Cut a few small holes near the bottom of the bottle.
- ✓ Place some treats or kibble inside the bottle.
- ✓ Show the bottle to your dog and let them investigate.
- ✓ Encourage your dog to roll, paw, or manipulate the bottle to release the treats through the holes.
- ✓ Provide verbal cues and positive reinforcement as your dog successfully extracts the treats.
- ✓ You can adjust the difficulty by changing the size of the holes or adding additional bottles for more challenging play.

DIY Snuffle Mat

A snuffle mat provides mental stimulation and engages your dog's sense of smell while encouraging problem-solving.

Step-by-step guide:
- ✓ Take a rubber mat or piece of fabric with a textured surface.
- ✓ Cut several long strips of fabric and tie them securely onto the mat.
- ✓ Sprinkle small treats or kibble pieces into the strips of fabric, hiding them from plain sight.
- ✓ Present the snuffle mat to your dog and let them explore.

- ✓ Encourage your dog to use their nose to sniff out and extract the hidden treats from the fabric strips.
- ✓ Celebrate your dog's success and provide praise as they find the treats.
- ✓ Gradually increase the difficulty by hiding the treats deeper within the fabric strips or adding more strips to make it more challenging.

ENGAGING YOUR DOG'S SENSES FOR MENTAL STIMULATION

Dogs rely on their senses of smell, sight, hearing, touch, and taste to navigate the world around them. By incorporating sensory-based exercises and activities into your dog's routine, you can stimulate their cognitive abilities, promote a healthy and active lifestyle, and strengthen the bond between you and your furry companion. This section explores various exercises and provides step-by-step guides to engage your dog's senses for mental stimulation.

SMELL

➢ Scent Work

Step-by-step guide:
- ✓ Start by introducing your dog to a specific scent, such as a small vial of essential oil or a specific plant.
- ✓ Encourage your dog to sniff and investigate the scent.
- ✓ Hide the scent in various locations around your home or outdoor area.
- ✓ Release your dog and give them a verbal cue, such as "Find it" or "Search."
- ✓ Allow your dog to follow their nose and locate the hidden scent.
- ✓ Reward your dog with treats, praise, or play when they successfully find the scent.
- ✓ Gradually increase the difficulty by hiding the scent in more challenging locations or using different scents.

➢ Sniffing Walks

Step-by-step guide:

- ✓ Take your dog on a walk in an area with different smells, such as a park or forest.
- ✓ Allow your dog to sniff and explore the environment at their own pace.
- ✓ Encourage your dog to engage their sense of smell by letting them stop and investigate interesting scents.
- ✓ Observe your dog's behavior and take note of their reactions to different smells.
- ✓ Vary your walking routes to provide new and stimulating scents for your dog to explore.

SIGHT

➢ Food Tracking

Step-by-step guide:
- ✓ Have your dog sit and stay while you place a few treats or pieces of kibble in plain sight.
- ✓ Release your dog from the stay command and encourage them to find and eat the treats.
- ✓ Gradually increase the difficulty by placing treats in more challenging hiding spots or areas with distractions.
- ✓ As your dog becomes more skilled, hide treats behind objects or partially under things to make it more visually challenging.

➢ Toy or Object Discrimination

Step-by-step guide:
- ✓ Gather a few different toys or objects with distinct visual characteristics.
- ✓ Show your dog one of the toys or objects and give it a specific cue or name.
- ✓ Repeat the process with each toy or object, associating them with different cues or names.
- ✓ Place the toys or objects in front of your dog and ask them to bring you a specific one based on the cue or name you provide.
- ✓ Praise and reward your dog when they bring you the correct toy or object.

- ✓ Increase the difficulty by introducing more toys or objects and asking your dog to discriminate between them based on visual cues.

HEARING

➢ Sound Recognition

Step-by-step guide:
- ✓ Select a specific sound or cue, such as a hand clap or whistle.
- ✓ Pair the sound with a reward, such as a treat or playtime.
- ✓ Repeat this process several times to help your dog associate the sound with a positive outcome.
- ✓ Test your dog's recognition by making the sound and rewarding them when they respond or look towards the source of the sound.
- ✓ Gradually increase the difficulty by making the sound in different locations or when your dog is engaged in other activities.

TOUCH

➢ Tactile Games

Step-by-step guide:
- ✓ Use a variety of objects with different textures, such as soft fabric, rubber, or different surfaces.
- ✓ Encourage your dog to interact with the objects using their paws, nose, or body.
- ✓ Incorporate playtime by playing gentle tug-of war with a soft toy or using a textured ball for fetch.
- ✓ Rotate and introduce new tactile toys or objects regularly to provide a variety of touch experiences.

TASTE

➢ Food Puzzle Toys

Step-by-step guide:

- ✓ Select a food puzzle toy that is suitable for your dog's size and eating habits.
- ✓ Fill the toy with their regular kibble or treats.
- ✓ Demonstrate to your dog how to manipulate the toy to access the food.
- ✓ Encourage your dog to engage with the toy and solve the puzzle to obtain their meal or treats.
- ✓ Supervise your dog during the activity to ensure their safety and enjoyment.

PART 3

ENRICHMENT ACTIVITIES FOR MENTAL STIMULATION

Chapter 1:

Scent Games and Nose Work

THE POWER OF A DOG'S SENSE OF SMELL

A dog's sense of smell is a remarkable and awe-inspiring ability that sets them apart from other animals. It is estimated that dogs possess a sense of smell between 10,000 to 100,000 times more sensitive than that of humans. Their olfactory system allows them to detect and discriminate odors with incredible precision. This remarkable sense of smell enables dogs to perform various tasks, from tracking missing persons to detecting diseases in humans.

➢ **Biological Mechanisms**

A dog's sense of smell begins with the nose, which is equipped with a complex network of olfactory receptors. These receptors capture odor molecules present in the environment and send signals to the olfactory bulb in the brain. Unlike humans, dogs possess a large olfactory bulb, which allows for greater processing of scent-related information.

Moreover, dogs have a specialized structure called the vomeronasal organ, also known as Jacobson's organ. This organ is responsible for detecting pheromones, chemical signals that convey important information between individuals of the same species. The combination of olfactory receptors and the vomeronasal organ gives dogs an unparalleled ability to detect and interpret scents.

➢ **Applications in Search and Rescue**

One of the most remarkable applications of a dog's sense of smell is in search and rescue operations. Trained search and rescue dogs can locate missing persons even in the most challenging conditions. Dogs can follow a person's scent trail, which consists of microscopic particles of skin cells and sweat that are shed naturally. These scent particles can remain in the environment for extended periods, allowing dogs to track individuals over long distances and even through water.

In disaster scenarios, such as earthquakes or avalanches, where time is of the essence, search and rescue dogs can swiftly locate survivors buried under rubble or snow. Their ability to pinpoint the exact location of a trapped person significantly increases the chances of a successful rescue.

➢ **Medical Applications**

The exceptional sense of smell possessed by dogs has found valuable applications in the medical field. Dogs can be trained to detect specific odors associated with various diseases, such as cancer, diabetes, and seizures. Research has shown that certain diseases can produce unique metabolic byproducts or volatile organic compounds that are detectable by dogs.

In the case of cancer detection, dogs have demonstrated an astonishing ability to detect cancer cells or the distinct odor signature associated with certain types of cancer. They can detect these odors in samples of breath, urine, or even directly from a person's skin. Although the exact mechanisms are still being studied, it is believed that dogs can identify the specific chemical changes occurring in the body due to the presence of diseases.

These abilities have led to the development of "medical detection dogs" that can be trained to detect diseases at an early stage. This has the potential to revolutionize medical diagnostics, as it offers a non-invasive and cost-effective method of early detection that can complement existing medical tests.

TEACHING SCENT DISCRIMINATION AND TRACKING GAMES

Teaching scent discrimination and tracking games to dogs not only taps into their natural abilities but also provides mental stimulation and strengthens the bond between dog and owner. These activities allow dogs to engage their powerful sense of smell while honing their focus and problem-solving skills.

Benefits of Scent Discrimination and Tracking Games

Engaging dogs in scent discrimination and tracking games offers numerous benefits for both their physical and mental well-being. These activities provide mental stimulation, which is crucial for preventing boredom and destructive behavior. By using their sense of smell to locate specific scents or track a trail, dogs exercise their cognitive abilities and enhance their problem-solving skills.

Furthermore, scent discrimination and tracking games offer an outlet for a dog's natural instincts and provide an opportunity to strengthen the bond between dog and owner. Dogs have an innate desire to explore and search for scents, and participating in these games allows them to fulfill this instinct in a controlled and rewarding manner. It also encourages communication and teamwork between the dog and their handler, promoting trust and mutual understanding.

Training Process for Scent Discrimination and Tracking Games

➢ Start with basic scent introduction: Begin by introducing your dog to a specific scent, such as a cotton pad scented with an essential oil or a specific item that carries a distinct smell. Allow your dog to investigate and associate the scent with positive experiences, such as treats or praise. Repeat this process multiple times to build a strong association between the scent and a reward.

➢ Introduce scent discrimination: Once your dog has established a positive association with a specific scent, you can begin teaching them to discriminate between different scents. Start with two scents, placing them in separate containers or hiding spots. Encourage your dog to sniff each container or spot and reward them when they

46

correctly identify the target scent. Gradually increase the number of scents and the difficulty of the discrimination task as your dog becomes more proficient.

➤ Teach tracking games: Tracking games involve following a scent trail left by a person or object. Begin by creating a simple trail using treats or a scented item. Allow your dog to observe you laying the trail, then give them the command to "track" or "find." Encourage them to follow the scent trail, praising and rewarding them along the way. Increase the complexity of the trail by adding turns, crossings, and obstacles as your dog becomes more skilled.

➤ Advanced tracking exercises: Once your dog has mastered the basics, you can advance to more challenging tracking exercises. This may include tracking longer trails, following trails in different environments (e.g., woods, urban areas), or introducing distractions along the way. Gradually increase the difficulty to keep your dog engaged and challenged.

Here are some exercises for teaching scent discrimination and tracking:

➤ **Scent Introduction**
  ✓ Choose a specific scent, such as an essential oil or a scented item.
  ✓ Allow your dog to sniff and investigate the scent while providing treats or praise.
  ✓ Repeat this process several times to establish a positive association between the scent and rewards.

➤ **Basic Discrimination**
  ✓ Prepare two containers, one with the target scent and another with a different scent or no scent.
  ✓ Encourage your dog to sniff both containers and reward them when they identify the container with the target scent correctly.

- ✓ Gradually increase the number of containers and scents as your dog becomes more proficient.
- ✓ Scent Line-Up
- ✓ Line up several containers with different scents, including the target scent.
- ✓ Instruct your dog to sniff each container and identify the one with the target scent.
- ✓ Reward your dog when they correctly indicate the container with the target scent.

➢ Hidden Scent
- ✓ Hide a container with the target scent among other containers or objects.
- ✓ Encourage your dog to search and identify the container with the target scent.
- ✓ Reward your dog when they successfully locate the hidden scent.

➢ Discrimination with Distractions
- ✓ Introduce distractions, such as different scents or food items, alongside the target scent.
- ✓ Instruct your dog to find the container or item with the target scent amidst the distractions.
- ✓ Reward your dog for correctly discriminating the target scent.

➢ Tracking with Treats
- ✓ Lay a simple scent trail using treats, placing them at regular intervals.
- ✓ Allow your dog to observe you laying the trail, then give the command to "track" or "find."
- ✓ Encourage your dog to follow the scent trail, praising and rewarding them when they reach each treat.

➢ **Longer Scent Trails**
- ✓ Increase the length of the scent trail gradually, placing treats or scented items at various points along the trail.
- ✓ Instruct your dog to track the scent trail and reward them when they successfully follow it to the end.

➢ **Tracking in Different Environments**
- ✓ Take your dog to different locations, such as parks or urban areas, to introduce tracking in various environments.
- ✓ Lay scent trails in these different environments and encourage your dog to track them.
- ✓ Provide rewards and praise when your dog successfully tracks in each environment.

➢ **Complex Tracking Trails**
- ✓ Create more challenging scent trails by adding turns, crossings, or loops.
- ✓ Guide your dog to navigate through these complex trails, rewarding them for staying on track and successfully following the scent.

➢ **Tracking with Aging Trails**
- ✓ Allow the scent trail to age for a certain period, from a few minutes to hours, before allowing your dog to track it.
- ✓ Instruct your dog to track the aged scent trail, rewarding them for successfully following it despite the time lapse.

INCORPORATING NOSE WORK INTO EVERYDAY LIFE

Nose work, also known as scent work, is a popular canine activity that engages a dog's powerful sense of smell. It involves teaching dogs to search for specific scents and identify their source. While nose work is often associated with organized competitions or formal training sessions, it can also be incorporated into everyday life as a fun and enriching activity for dogs.

Benefits of Nose Work

Incorporating nose work into everyday life offers several benefits for both dogs and their owners.

➤ Mental Stimulation: Nose work engages a dog's cognitive abilities, providing mental stimulation that helps prevent boredom and destructive behaviors. It challenges their problem-solving skills as they search for and identify specific scents.

➤ Physical Exercise: Searching for scents requires physical activity, such as sniffing, exploring, and navigating various environments. This form of mental and physical exercise contributes to a dog's overall well-being and can help expend excess energy.

➤ Bonding and Communication: Engaging in nose work activities with your dog strengthens the bond and communication between you. It requires teamwork and trust as you work together to solve scent-related challenges.

➤ Confidence Building: Successfully finding and identifying scents boosts a dog's confidence and self-esteem. The sense of accomplishment they experience during nose work activities can have a positive impact on their overall behavior and well-being.

➤ Stress Reduction: Nose work taps into a dog's natural instincts and provides a constructive outlet for their energy. It can help reduce anxiety and stress by allowing them to focus their attention and energy on a rewarding activity.

Practical Ways to Incorporate Nose Work

➤ **Interactive Feeding**

Transform mealtime into a nose work activity by scattering your dog's kibble or hiding it in various locations.

Step-by-step guide:

- ✓ Instead of using a traditional food bowl, scatter your dog's kibble on the floor or in a specific area.
- ✓ Encourage your dog to use their sense of smell to find and eat the scattered food.
- ✓ Gradually increase the difficulty by scattering the kibble in more challenging locations or by using puzzle toys to hide the food.

> **Hide-and-Seek**

Engage in a game of hide-and-seek with your dog using their favorite toys or treats.

Step-by-step guide:

- ✓ Have your dog sit or stay in one room while you hide a toy or treat in another room or area of your house.
- ✓ Release your dog and give them a cue, such as "Find it" or "Search," to start searching for the hidden item.
- ✓ Celebrate and reward your dog when they successfully locate the hidden item.
- ✓ Gradually increase the difficulty by hiding items in more challenging locations or using scent cues to guide your dog to the hidden objects.

> **Scented Toy Search**

Introduce scent to your dog's toys and encourage them to search for and retrieve the scented toys.

Step-by-step guide:

- ✓ Rub a small amount of essential oil or use a scent kit specifically designed for dog nose work to add scent to your dog's toys.
- ✓ Place the scented toys in a designated area or hide them in various locations around the house or yard.
- ✓ Encourage your dog to use their sense of smell to search for and retrieve the scented toys.

✓ Reward your dog with praise or treats when they find and interact with the scented toys.

➤ **Outdoor Scent Trails**

Create simple scent trails for your dog to follow during walks or outdoor adventures.

Step-by-step guide:
✓ Before going for a walk, prepare treats or scented items that your dog can follow.
✓ Drop treats or place scented items, such as cotton pads with essential oil, at intervals along the route.
✓ Allow your dog to use their sense of smell to follow the scent trail and find the treats or scented objects.
✓ Celebrate and reward your dog when they successfully track and find the scented items.
✓ Gradually increase the complexity of the scent trails by making them longer or adding turns and obstacles.

➤ **Find the Treat**

Hide treats or favorite toys in different areas of your home or yard and encourage your dog to search for them using their sense of smell.

Step-by-step guide:
✓ Begin by hiding treats or toys in relatively easy-to-find locations.
✓ Encourage your dog to search for the hidden items using their nose.
✓ Use verbal cues, such as "Find it" or "Search," to direct your dog towards the hidden treasures.
✓ Reward your dog with praise or additional treats when they successfully locate the hidden items.
✓ Increase the difficulty by hiding items in more challenging spots or using scent cues to guide your dog.

➢ **Scented Blanket or Pillow**

Introduce a specific scent to a blanket or pillow and encourage your dog to locate and interact with the scented item.

Step-by-step guide:
- ✓ Choose a blanket or pillow that your dog is familiar with.
- ✓ Rub a small amount of essential oil or use a scent spray on the blanket or pillow to introduce the scent.
- ✓ Place the scented item in a designated area or hide it in various locations.
- ✓ Encourage your dog to use their sense of smell to locate and interact with the scented item.
- ✓ Reward your dog with praise or treats when they successfully find and engage with the scented blanket or pillow.

➢ **DIY Scent Detection Stations**

Create scent detection stations in your home by hiding scented cotton pads, containers with scents, or scented objects.

Step-by-step guide:
- ✓ Prepare scented cotton pads by adding a few drops of essential oil or using scent kits specifically designed for dog nose work.
- ✓ Hide the scented cotton pads, containers with scents, or scented objects in different rooms or areas of your home.
- ✓ Encourage your dog to search for and identify the scent at each station.
- ✓ Use rewards and praise when your dog successfully locates and indicates the scented items.
- ✓ Vary the difficulty by using different scents or increasing the number of scent detection stations.

➢ **Outdoor Treasure Hunt**

Set up an outdoor treasure hunt for your dog by hiding toys, treats, or scented objects in your yard or a nearby park.

Step-by-step guide:
- ✓ Hide toys, treats, or scented objects in various locations in your yard or a nearby park.
- ✓ Provide your dog with a cue, such as "Find it" or "Search," to start searching for the hidden treasures.
- ✓ Encourage your dog to use their sense of smell to locate and retrieve the hidden items.
- ✓ Celebrate and reward your dog when they successfully find and interact with the hidden treasures.
- ✓ Increase the difficulty by hiding items in more challenging spots or using scent cues to guide your dog.

➢ **Car Scent Identification**

Introduce different scents to objects associated with car rides, such as car keys or seat covers, and encourage your dog to identify and indicate the scented object.

Step-by-step guide:
- ✓ Select different scents, such as essential oils or specific fragrances, to associate with car-related experiences.
- ✓ Apply the scents to objects like car keys, seat covers, or car air fresheners.
- ✓ Present the scented objects to your dog and encourage them to identify and indicate the object with the specific scent.
- ✓ Reward your dog for correctly identifying the scented object and reinforce the association between the scent and car-related experiences.
- ✓ Gradually increase the number of scents and objects for your dog to discriminate between.

➤ **Scented Puzzles and Toys**

Invest in interactive puzzle toys or treat-dispensing toys that can be scented, providing mental stimulation and encouraging your dog to use their sense of smell.

Step-by-step guide:

- ✓ Select puzzle toys or treat-dispensing toys that are designed to be scented.
- ✓ Fill these toys with treats or use scent kits to introduce specific scents to the toys.
- ✓ Present the scented toys to your dog and encourage them to solve the puzzle or manipulate the toy to access the rewards.
- ✓ Celebrate and reward your dog when they successfully engage with the scented puzzles and toys.
- ✓ Increase the complexity of the puzzles or the difficulty of accessing the treats as your dog becomes more proficient.

Remember to adapt the difficulty level of these activities based on your dog's skill level and gradually increase the challenge as they become more comfortable and proficient in using their sense of smell.

Chapter 2:

DIY Enrichment Projects

HOMEMADE PUZZLE TOYS AND TREAT DISPENSERS

Homemade puzzle toys can be made from simple materials you already have at home, such as cardboard boxes or plastic bottles, saving you money compared to purchasing commercial puzzle toys. By making your own puzzle toys, you also have the flexibility to customize them according to your dog's size, skill level, and preferences. You can adjust the difficulty level, size of openings, or type of treats used to suit your dog's needs.

Here's a step-by-step guide on how to make homemade puzzle toys and treat dispensers:

➢ **Water Bottle Treat Dispenser**

Materials:
- ✓ Empty plastic water bottle
- ✓ Scissors
- ✓ Treats or kibble

Steps:
- ✓ Remove the label from the water bottle and clean it thoroughly.
- ✓ Make small holes in the sides of the bottle using scissors. Ensure the holes are large enough for treats to fall out.
- ✓ Fill the bottle with your dog's favorite treats or kibble.
- ✓ Replace the bottle cap tightly.
- ✓ Show the treat-filled bottle to your dog and let them figure out how to roll and manipulate it to release the treats.

➤ Cardboard Box Puzzle

Materials:

- ✓ Cardboard box (various sizes)
- ✓ Scissors
- ✓ Treats or kibble

Steps:

- ✓ Take a cardboard box and cut several holes of different sizes on the sides. You can use scissors to make the holes.
- ✓ Place treats or kibble inside the box.
- ✓ Fold the flaps of the box closed or tape them shut to create a challenge for your dog.
- ✓ Present the box to your dog and let them explore and figure out how to retrieve the treats through the holes.

➤ PVC Pipe Treat Dispenser

Materials:

- ✓ PVC pipes (various sizes)
- ✓ Saw or PVC pipe cutter
- ✓ Treats or kibble

Steps:

- ✓ Cut the PVC pipes into several short sections using a saw or PVC pipe cutter. The sections should be long enough for treats to fit inside.
- ✓ Seal one end of each PVC pipe section with duct tape or glue.
- ✓ Fill the pipes with treats or kibble.
- ✓ Seal the other end of each pipe.
- ✓ Scatter the filled PVC pipe sections in an open area and let your dog figure out how to extract the treats from inside.

➢ **Muffin Tin Treat Game**

Materials:

✓ Muffin tin or ice cube tray

✓ Tennis balls or similar toys

✓ Treats or kibble

Steps:

✓ Place a treat or a small amount of kibble in each compartment of the muffin tin or ice cube tray.

✓ Cover each compartment with tennis balls or similar toys.

✓ Present the treat-filled muffin tin or ice cube tray to your dog and encourage them to find and remove the balls to access the treats underneath.

➢ **Treat-Inside-Box Game**

Materials:

✓ Cardboard box

✓ Scissors

✓ Treats or kibble

Steps:

✓ Cut several small holes on the sides of the cardboard box.

✓ Place treats or kibble inside the box.

✓ Close the box and seal it with tape or glue.

✓ Encourage your dog to use their paws, nose, or teeth to find and retrieve the treats through the holes in the box.

CREATING INDOOR AND OUTDOOR SCAVENGER HUNTS

Scavenger hunts engage your dog's brain and provide mental exercise. Searching for hidden items or following scent trails stimulates their natural instincts and requires problem-solving skills. This mental stimulation helps keep your dog sharp, focused, and mentally engaged. It also helps burn off excess energy, promotes physical fitness, and can be especially beneficial for dogs with high energy levels or those who may not have access to extensive outdoor exercise areas.

- ➢ **DIY Indoor Scavenger Hunt**

  Materials:
  - ✓ Dog treats or toys
  - ✓ Boxes or containers (optional)
  - ✓ Sticky notes or index cards
  - ✓ Pen or marker

  Instructions:
  - ✓ Determine the Location: Choose a specific area in your home where you want to set up the scavenger hunt, such as the living room, hallway, or a designated play area.
  - ✓ Plan the Clues: Write down a series of clues on sticky notes or index cards. Each clue should lead your dog to the next hiding spot.
  - ✓ Hide the Clues: Place the clues strategically in different locations around the designated area. Make sure they are visible and easily accessible to your dog.
  - ✓ Hide Treats or Toys: Along with each clue, hide a treat or toy for your dog to find. You can hide them behind furniture, under blankets, inside boxes, or any other creative hiding spots.
  - ✓ Start the Scavenger Hunt: Begin the scavenger hunt by presenting the first clue to your dog. Encourage them to sniff and explore the area to find the hidden treats or toys.
  - ✓ Follow the Clues: As your dog finds each treat or toy, guide them to the next clue using verbal cues or pointing. Celebrate their success and offer praise or additional rewards.
  - ✓ Optional Challenges: To make the scavenger hunt more engaging, you can incorporate additional challenges such as obstacle courses or puzzle toys along the way.

> **DIY Outdoor Scavenger Hunt**

Materials:

✓ Dog treats or toys

✓ Scented cotton pads or essential oils (optional)

✓ Flags or markers (optional)

✓ Leash and harness (if necessary)

Instructions:

✓ Choose the Outdoor Area: Select a safe and dog-friendly outdoor location such as a backyard, a park, or a nature trail.

✓ Determine the Scavenger Items: Decide on the items your dog will search for during the scavenger hunt. It can be specific objects or scents.

✓ Hide the Items: Hide treats or toys at various locations throughout the outdoor area. If using scents, place scented cotton pads or add a few drops of essential oil to specific spots.

✓ Set Up Markers (optional): If you want to create a designated route, you can place flags or markers along the path to guide your dog from one location to another.

✓ Start the Scavenger Hunt: Begin by leading your dog to the first location or providing them with the first scent. Use verbal cues or gestures to encourage them to search and find the hidden items.

✓ Encourage and Reward: Support your dog's search by offering encouragement and praise. Reward them with treats or playtime when they successfully find the hidden items.

✓ Increase the Challenge: As your dog becomes more proficient, make the hiding spots more difficult or introduce additional scents or objects to search for.

Remember to prioritize your dog's safety during outdoor scavenger hunts. Keep them on a leash if necessary, supervise their exploration, and ensure the hiding spots are free from any potential hazards.

BUILDING AN AGILITY COURSE AT HOME

Agility courses consist of various obstacles and challenges that test your dog's agility, coordination, and obedience skills. Creating your own agility course allows you to customize it according to your dog's abilities and space available.

Here are a few examples of DIY agility course exercises:

Exercise 1: Hurdle Jumps

Materials:
- ✓ PVC pipes or wooden poles
- ✓ Connectors or brackets
- ✓ Measuring tape

Instructions:
- ✓ Measure and cut the PVC pipes or wooden poles to the desired length for the jumps. A typical height for beginners is around 8-12 inches.
- ✓ Attach the pipes or poles to the connectors or brackets to create the jump bars.
- ✓ Set up the jumps in a line, leaving enough space between each jump for your dog to clear.

How to Use:
- ✓ Begin by guiding your dog to the starting point of the jump line.
- ✓ Use a treat or toy to encourage your dog to jump over each hurdle.
- ✓ Start with lower heights and gradually increase the height as your dog becomes more confident and skilled.
- ✓ Use positive reinforcement and praise your dog for successfully clearing each jump.

Exercise 2: Tunnel Run

Materials:
- ✓ PVC pipes or flexible tunnel material
- ✓ Sandbags or weights

Instructions:
- ✓ Create a curved tunnel shape by connecting the PVC pipes or using flexible tunnel material.
- ✓ Secure the ends of the tunnel with sandbags or weights to prevent movement.
- ✓ Place the tunnel in a straight line or incorporate curves based on the available space.

How to Use:
- ✓ Entice your dog with a treat or toy to enter one end of the tunnel.
- ✓ Encourage them to run through the tunnel to reach the other end.
- ✓ Start with a straight tunnel and then introduce curves to increase the challenge.
- ✓ Use positive reinforcement and reward your dog for successfully completing the tunnel run.

Exercise 3: Weave Poles

Materials:
- ✓ PVC pipes or thin poles
- ✓ Drill
- ✓ Measuring tape

Instructions:
- ✓ Measure and mark equal intervals along the length of the PVC pipes or poles. Start with a larger gap between the poles for beginners.
- ✓ Use a drill to create holes at the marked intervals.

- Insert the poles into the ground, leaving enough space between them for your dog to weave through.

How to Use:
- Begin with your dog on one side of the weave poles.
- Encourage them to navigate through the poles, weaving in and out.
- Start with a small number of poles and gradually increase as your dog becomes more proficient.
- Use treats or toys as rewards for successfully completing the weave poles.

Exercise 4: Tire Jump

Materials:
- Hula hoop or small tire
- Rope or string
- Hooks or supports

Instructions:
- Attach the hula hoop or tire to a rope or string.
- Hang the rope or string from hooks or supports at an appropriate height for your dog.

How to Use:
- Guide your dog to the starting point of the tire jump.
- Encourage them to jump through the tire hoop, using treats or toys as motivation.
- Start with a larger hoop diameter and lower height for beginners and gradually increase the challenge.
- Reward your dog with positive reinforcement for successfully jumping through the tire.

PART 4

ADVANCED

MENTAL EXERCISES

Chapter 1:

Tricks and Advanced Skills

TEACHING IMPRESSIVE TRICKS TO CHALLENGE THE MIND

Teaching impressive tricks goes beyond simple obedience commands. It allows you to delve into a realm of creativity, communication, and trust-building with your furry companion.

Impressive tricks serve as mental puzzles for your dog, stimulating their cognitive abilities and providing them with the mental exercise they need to stay sharp and engaged. These tricks are not only entertaining to watch but also offer a remarkable opportunity for you and your dog to bond on a deeper level.

Trick 1: High Five

Steps:

➢ Start with your dog in a sitting position in front of you.

➢ Hold a treat in your closed fist, showing it to your dog.

➢ Slowly move your closed fist towards your dog's paw.

➢ As your dog reaches out to touch your fist with their paw, say "High Five" and open your hand to reveal the treat.

➢ Repeat this process several times, using the verbal cue "High Five" consistently.

➢ Gradually, start offering your hand without a treat, and reward your dog with a treat from your other hand when they perform the trick correctly.

➢ Practice regularly, gradually fading the use of treats and relying on the verbal cue and praise as the reward.

Trick 2: Spin

Steps:

➢ Start with your dog in a standing position in front of you.

➢ Hold a treat near their nose and slowly move it in a circular motion.

➢ As your dog follows the treat, their body will naturally turn in a circular motion.

➢ Once they complete the spin, say "Spin" and give them the treat as a reward.

➢ Repeat the process in the opposite direction, using the verbal cue "Spin" consistently.

➢ Practice regularly, gradually fading the use of treats and relying on the verbal cue and praise as the reward.

Trick 3: Play Dead

Steps:

➢ Start with your dog in a lying down position on their side.

➢ Hold a treat near their nose and slowly move it towards their shoulder, guiding them to roll onto their back.

➢ As they roll onto their back, say "Play Dead" and give them the treat as a reward.

➢ Repeat this process several times, using the verbal cue "Play Dead" consistently.

➢ Gradually, start offering the treat from your other hand, positioned near their mouth, as if they were taking it while lying on their back.

➢ Practice regularly, gradually fading the use of treats and relying on the verbal cue and praise as the reward.

Trick 4: Take a Bow

Steps:

➤ Start with your dog in a standing position in front of you.

➤ Hold a treat in front of their nose, guiding them downward.

➤ As their front legs lower and their head goes towards the ground, say "Take a Bow" and give them the treat as a reward.

➤ Repeat this process several times, using the verbal cue "Take a Bow" consistently.

➤ Gradually, start offering the treat from your other hand, positioned near their mouth, as if they were taking it while in the bow position.

➤ Practice regularly, gradually fading the use of treats and relying on the verbal cue and praise as the reward.

Trick 5: Roll Over

Steps:

➤ Start with your dog in a lying down position.

➤ Hold a treat close to their nose and move it towards their shoulder, encouraging them to roll onto their side.

➤ As they roll onto their side, continue moving the treat in a circular motion, guiding them to roll onto their back.

➤ Once they complete the full roll, say "Roll Over" and give them the treat as a reward.

➤ Repeat this process several times, using the verbal cue "Roll Over" consistently.

➤ Gradually, start offering the treat from your other hand, positioned near their mouth, as if they were taking it while in the rolled position.

> Practice regularly, gradually fading the use of treats and relying on the verbal cue and praise as the reward.

Trick 6: Crawl

Steps:

> Start with your dog in a down position.

> Hold a treat near their nose and slowly move it forward, just out of their reach.

> As they stretch forward to follow the treat, say "Crawl" and reward them with the treat.

> Repeat this process, gradually increasing the distance your dog needs to crawl before receiving the treat.

> Use a mat or towel on the floor to guide them and provide a visual cue for crawling.

> Practice regularly, gradually fading the use of treats and relying on the verbal cue and praise as the reward.

Trick 7: Balance Treat on Nose

Steps:

> Start with your dog in a sitting position.

> Hold a treat in your hand and place it on your dog's nose.

> Give the verbal cue "Balance" and hold the treat for a few seconds.

> Release the treat by giving the command "Okay" or a similar release cue, allowing your dog to catch it in their mouth.

> Repeat this process, gradually increasing the duration of balancing the treat on their nose.

> Practice regularly, gradually fading the use of treats and relying on the verbal cue and praise as the reward.

Trick 8: Paws Up

Steps:

➤ Start with your dog in a standing position in front of an object, such as a low platform or a step stool.

➤ Hold a treat in your hand and guide your dog to place their front paws on the object.

➤ As they place their paws on the object, say "Paws Up" and reward them with the treat.

➤ Repeat this process, gradually increasing the height of the object or introducing different objects for them to place their paws on.

➤ Practice regularly, gradually fading the use of treats and relying on the verbal cue and praise as the reward.

ADVANCED OBEDIENCE AND OFF-LEASH TRAINING

Advanced obedience and off-leash training require a solid foundation in basic obedience commands and a gradual progression to off-leash work. It is crucial to prioritize safety and take the necessary precautions when training your dog off-leash. Here is a step-by-step guide to advanced obedience and off-leash training:

➤ **Master Basic Obedience Commands**

Before moving to advanced training, ensure your dog is proficient in basic obedience commands such as sit, stay, down, come, and heel. These commands will serve as building blocks for advanced training.

➤ **Build a Strong Relationship**

Strengthen your bond with your dog through positive reinforcement, consistent training, and regular exercise. A strong relationship based on trust and respect will make advanced training more effective.

➢ **Choose a Safe Training Area**

Select a secure and enclosed area for off-leash training. This could be a fenced backyard, a dog park, or any other controlled environment where your dog can't run off and there are minimal distractions.

➢ **Use a Long Training Lead**

Introduce a long training lead (about 20 to 30 feet) to give your dog freedom to move while still maintaining control. This will serve as a safety measure during off-leash training.

➢ **Practice Recall on a Long Lead**

Begin off-leash training by practicing recall exercises using the long lead. Start in a low-distraction environment and call your dog's name followed by the "come" command. Use positive reinforcement (treats, praise) when your dog responds correctly.

➢ **Gradually Increase Distance**

Over time, gradually increase the distance between you and your dog when practicing recall. Begin with short distances and gradually work up to longer distances. This helps build your dog's confidence and reinforces reliable recall.

➢ **Introduce Distractions**

Gradually introduce distractions during off-leash training. Start with mild distractions, such as toys or low-level noises, and gradually progress to more challenging distractions like other dogs or people.

➢ **Reinforce Off-Leash Commands**

Reinforce off-leash commands such as sit, stay, and heel. Practice these commands in a controlled off-leash environment, gradually increasing the duration and distance of each command.

> ## Use Positive Reinforcement

Continue using positive reinforcement techniques throughout the training process. Reward your dog with treats, praise, or play whenever they successfully follow commands, respond to recalls, or exhibit good behavior.

> ## Monitor Progress and Gradually Remove the Lead

Monitor your dog's progress during off-leash training. If your dog consistently responds well to commands and recalls, gradually decrease your reliance on the long lead until your dog can be trusted off-leash.

> ## Consistency and Continued Practice

Consistency is key to successful advanced obedience and off-leash training. Regularly practice commands, recalls, and off-leash work with your dog to maintain and reinforce their training.

Remember, off-leash training should only be attempted in safe and controlled environments, and the timing for transitioning to off-leash work may vary depending on your dog's individual progress. If you encounter any challenges or your dog shows signs of disobedience or unsafe behavior, consider consulting a professional dog trainer for guidance.

INCORPORATING MENTAL STIMULATION IN CANINE SPORTS

Canine sports are not only great for physical exercise but also play a crucial role in mental stimulation for dogs. Engaging in sports activities not only helps to alleviate boredom but also provides an outlet for their energy and promotes a healthy bond between dogs and their owners. Here, we will explore several canine sports that offer mental stimulation and provide detailed instructions on how to engage in each activity effectively. Whether you have an energetic working breed or a small companion dog, there is a sport suitable for every dog's needs.

Agility

Agility is a popular sport that involves navigating a course with various obstacles, such as jumps, tunnels, and weave poles. It requires dogs to focus, follow commands, and make split-second decisions. Here's how to get started:

Equipment:

- ✓ Agility course with jumps, tunnels, and weave poles
- ✓ Treats or toys as rewards
- ✓ A clicker (optional)

Instructions:

- ➢ Teach basic obedience commands: Before starting agility, ensure your dog understands basic commands such as "sit," "stay," "come," and "heel."

- ➢ Introduce agility equipment gradually: Begin by introducing one obstacle at a time. Use treats or toys to encourage your dog to navigate the obstacle and reward them for success.

- ➢ Build up to full courses: Once your dog is comfortable with individual obstacles, start connecting them to form a complete course. Guide your dog through the course using verbal cues, hand signals, and rewards.

- ➢ Increase difficulty gradually: Once your dog is confident with basic courses, add challenges like different heights for jumps or increasing the speed. This will keep them mentally engaged and excited about the sport.

Nose Work

Nose work is a sport that taps into a dog's natural scenting abilities. It involves teaching dogs to locate specific scents hidden in containers or different environments. Here's how to get started:

Equipment:

- ✓ Scented objects (e.g., cotton swabs)
- ✓ Containers (such as boxes or tins)
- ✓ Treats or toys as rewards

Instructions:

- ➢ Introduce scent recognition: Start by associating a specific scent (e.g., a drop of essential oil) with a reward. Present the scent to your dog and reward them with a treat or playtime whenever they show interest.

- ➢ Hide scented objects: Place the scented object in one of several containers. Encourage your dog to find the container with the scent. When they succeed, reward them generously.

- ➢ Increase difficulty: Gradually increase the number of containers and the complexity of hiding spots. You can also introduce different scents to expand their scent recognition skills.

- ➢ Advanced nose work: Once your dog has mastered finding scents in containers, you can progress to searching for scents in various environments, such as indoors or outdoors. This will provide a more challenging and mentally stimulating experience for your dog.

Rally Obedience

Rally Obedience is a sport that combines elements of traditional obedience and agility. It involves following a course with different stations, where dogs perform specific obedience exercises. Here's how to get started:

Equipment:

- ✓ Rally course signs (can be purchased or printed)
- ✓ Treats or toys as rewards

✓ A clicker (optional)

Instructions:

➢ Teach basic obedience commands: Ensure your dog understands basic obedience commands like "sit," "stay," "down," "come," and "heel."

➢ Familiarize with rally signs: Introduce your dog to the rally course signs, associating each sign with the corresponding obedience exercise. Practice the exercises individually before combining them into a course.

➢ Practice on-leash skills: Begin practicing the rally course on-leash, guiding your dog through each station using verbal cues and hand signals. Reward your dog at each station for successful completion.

➢ Progress to off-leash skills: Once your dog is comfortable with on-leash exercises, gradually transition to off-leash work. Ensure your dog's reliability with commands before attempting off-leash rally obedience.

➢ Increase difficulty: Add variations to the exercises, such as changing the order of stations or introducing distractions. This will challenge your dog's ability to focus and follow commands.

Flyball

Flyball is a fast-paced relay race sport that involves teams of dogs competing against each other. The goal is for each dog to jump over a series of hurdles, retrieve a tennis ball from a box, and return to the starting line. Here's how to get started:

Equipment:

✓ Flyball box (a device that releases a tennis ball)
✓ Hurdles
✓ Tennis balls
✓ Treats or toys as rewards

Instructions:

➢ Build foundation skills: Teach your dog basic obedience commands like "sit," "stay," and "come." Additionally, work on their retrieving skills by encouraging them to fetch and return objects.

➢ Introduce the flyball box: Teach your dog to retrieve a tennis ball from the flyball box. Start with a stationary box, and gradually introduce the ball release mechanism. Reward your dog for successful retrieves.

➢ Add hurdles: Set up a series of low hurdles, and guide your dog to jump over them while heading towards the flyball box. Encourage them with treats or toys and reward them at the box for successful retrieves.

➢ Form a team: Once your dog is comfortable with the individual tasks, join a local flyball team or find other dog owners interested in forming a team. Practice relay races with other dogs, ensuring smooth handoffs between team members.

Treibball

Treibball, also known as "push ball," is a sport that originated in Germany. It involves herding large exercise balls into a goal using only verbal and hand signals. This sport provides mental stimulation and helps develop a dog's problem-solving skills. Here's how to get started:

Equipment:

✓ Large exercise balls
✓ Cones or markers to create a goal area
✓ Treats or toys as rewards

Instructions:

➤ Teach basic obedience commands: Ensure your dog understands basic commands like "sit," "stay," "come," and "heel." These commands will be essential for guiding your dog during treibball.

➤ Introduce the exercise balls: Teach your dog to touch and push the exercise ball with their nose or shoulder. Start by rewarding any interaction with the ball and gradually shape the behavior into intentional pushing.

➤ Create a goal area: Set up a goal area using cones or markers. Guide your dog to push the exercise ball into the goal area. Reward them for successful pushes and progress to using verbal cues and hand signals.

➤ Increase difficulty: Add more balls to the game and vary their placement. Introduce obstacles or create a course for your dog to navigate while herding the balls. This will challenge their problem-solving skills and ability to follow cues.

Canine Freestyle

Canine freestyle, also known as dog dancing, is a creative sport that combines obedience, tricks, and music. It involves choreographing routines with your dog and performing them to music. Here's how to get started:

Equipment:

✓ Music player and speakers
✓ Treats or toys as rewards
✓ Clicker (optional)

Instructions:

➤ Establish basic obedience skills: Ensure your dog understands basic obedience commands like "sit," "stay," "lie down," and "heel." These commands will form the foundation of your freestyle routine.

➢ Teach tricks and creative movements: Teach your dog a variety of tricks and creative movements such as spins, jumps, bows, and weaving through your legs. Use positive reinforcement and rewards to encourage and reinforce these behaviors.

➢ Choose music and choreograph routines: Select music that suits your dog's personality and energy level. Choreograph routines that incorporate a combination of obedience commands, tricks, and creative movements, synchronized with the music.

➢ Practice and refine routines: Practice the routines regularly, ensuring smooth transitions and precise timing with the music. Gradually increase the complexity and difficulty of the routines to keep your dog mentally engaged and challenged.

➢ Perform and have fun: Showcase your freestyle routine in front of an audience, whether it's at a local event, competition, or simply for friends and family. Remember to enjoy the experience and celebrate the bond between you and your dog.

Disc Dog

Disc dog, also known as Frisbee dog, is a sport that involves throwing discs for your dog to catch and perform various tricks and acrobatic maneuvers. It requires coordination, focus, and teamwork between you and your dog. Here's how to get started:

Equipment:

✓ Discs (appropriate for your dog's size and breed)
✓ Open space or a designated disc dog arena
✓ Treats or toys as rewards

Instructions:

➢ Teach basic obedience commands: Ensure your dog understands basic obedience commands like "sit," "stay," "come," and "fetch." These commands will be crucial for the disc dog training.

➤ Introduce the disc: Begin by introducing your dog to the disc and rewarding them for showing interest in it. Encourage them to grab and hold the disc using positive reinforcement.

➤ Teach catching and retrieving: Start by throwing the disc at a short distance and encourage your dog to catch it in the air or after it lands. Gradually increase the distance and height of the throws as your dog becomes more comfortable.

➤ Add tricks and acrobatics: Integrate tricks and acrobatic maneuvers into your disc dog routine, such as jumping catches, spins, flips, and weaving between your legs. Use treats and rewards to reinforce these behaviors.

➤ Practice freestyle routines: Choreograph sequences of throws, catches, and tricks to create a freestyle routine. Focus on creating smooth transitions and variety in your routine to showcase your dog's skills and athleticism.

Canicross

Canicross is a sport that combines running and hiking with your dog. It involves a human-dog team running together, connected by a waist belt and a bungee line. Canicross provides mental stimulation and physical exercise for both you and your dog. Here's how to get started:

Equipment:

✓ Canicross harness for your dog
✓ Waist belt and bungee line
✓ Proper running shoes and clothing for yourself
✓ Treats or toys as rewards

Instructions:

➤ Ensure your dog's fitness: Before starting canicross, ensure that your dog is physically fit for running. Consult with your veterinarian to ensure your dog is in good health and suitable for this type of activity.

➤ Introduce the equipment: Introduce your dog to the canicross harness and allow them to get accustomed to wearing it. Gradually attach the waist belt and bungee line, ensuring a comfortable fit for both you and your dog.

➤ Start with short runs: Begin with short, slow-paced runs to allow your dog to become familiar with running alongside you. Use positive reinforcement and rewards to encourage your dog to stay focused and maintain a steady pace.

➤ Build endurance gradually: Gradually increase the distance and intensity of your runs as your dog builds endurance. Pay attention to your dog's cues and adjust the pace accordingly to prevent overexertion.

➤ Focus on teamwork: Practice commands like "heel" and "hike" to establish communication and coordination between you and your dog. Encourage your dog to maintain a steady pace, and reward them for positive behavior and focus.

Chapter 2:

Cognitive Challenges and

Problem Solving

ADDRESSING BOREDOM AND DESTRUCTIVE BEHAVIORS

Boredom and destructive behaviors often go hand in hand for dogs. When dogs lack mental stimulation and proper outlets for their energy, they may resort to destructive behaviors as a way to alleviate their boredom. It's crucial to address these issues to ensure your dog's well-being and prevent damage to your home. These can be challenging to deal with, but with a systematic approach, you can address these issues effectively. It's important to understand the underlying causes of the behaviors and provide appropriate outlets for your dog's physical and mental needs.

➤ **Excessive Chewing**

Dogs may engage in excessive chewing when they are bored or seeking attention. They may target furniture, shoes, or other household items.

Step 1: Provide appropriate chew toys: Offer a variety of chew toys, such as durable rubber or nylon toys, to redirect your dog's chewing behavior. Encourage them to chew on these toys by making them more enticing through the use of treats or interactive features.

Step 2: Supervise and redirect: Keep a close eye on your dog and redirect their chewing behavior when you catch them chewing on inappropriate items. Replace the item with an appropriate chew toy and reward them for chewing on the toy instead.

Step 3: Increase mental stimulation: Address the underlying boredom by providing mental stimulation. Engage in activities like puzzle toys, treat-dispensing toys, or training sessions to keep your dog mentally engaged.

- ➤ **Digging**

Dogs may dig in the yard or indoor spaces due to boredom, excess energy, or a desire to escape.

Step 1: Create a designated digging area: Designate a specific area in your yard where your dog is allowed to dig. Fill it with loose soil or sand and bury toys or treats to encourage digging in that specific spot.

Step 2: Increase physical exercise: Ensure your dog gets enough physical exercise through walks, runs, or play sessions. A tired dog is less likely to engage in excessive digging.

Step 3: Provide mental stimulation: Engage in interactive games or provide puzzle toys to keep your dog mentally stimulated and reduce their desire to dig out of boredom.

Step 4: Block access to digging spots: If your dog has a particular area they dig in, block access to that area temporarily using fencing or other barriers until the behavior is under control.

- ➤ **Scratching Furniture**

Dogs may scratch furniture to alleviate boredom, mark their territory, or relieve stress.

Step 1: Provide appropriate scratching alternatives: Offer scratching posts or boards that are appealing to your dog. Use positive reinforcement to encourage them to use these alternatives instead of furniture. You can also sprinkle catnip or use scratching post attractants to make them more enticing.

Step 2: Redirect and discourage: When you catch your dog scratching furniture, redirect their attention to the appropriate scratching post. Use deterrents like double-sided tape or pet-safe sprays on furniture to discourage scratching.

Step 3: Increase mental and physical exercise: Ensure your dog is mentally and physically stimulated through interactive play, training sessions, or puzzle toys. A tired and mentally engaged dog is less likely to engage in destructive scratching.

➤ **Pacing and Restlessness**

Dogs may pace and display restlessness when they are bored, lack exercise, or have pent-up energy.

Step 1: Increase physical exercise: Provide regular opportunities for physical exercise through walks, runs, or active play sessions. Aim for a minimum of 30 minutes to an hour of exercise daily, depending on your dog's breed and energy level.

Step 2: Mental stimulation: Engage your dog in mentally stimulating activities like obedience training, scent games, puzzle toys, or interactive play sessions. This will help tire them mentally and alleviate boredom.

Step 3: Create a structured routine: Establish a consistent daily routine that includes designated times for exercise, feeding, play, and rest. Dogs thrive on routine and predictability.

Step 4: Provide a safe and comfortable space: Ensure your dog has a dedicated space where they feel safe and secure. Include comfortable bedding, interactive toys, and a calm environment where they can relax and unwind.

➤ **Separation Anxiety**

Dogs with separation anxiety may exhibit destructive behaviors when left alone, such as excessive barking, chewing, or scratching.

Step 1: Gradual departures and arrivals: Make your departures and arrivals low-key to avoid triggering anxiety. Avoid making a big fuss when leaving or returning home.

Step 2: Desensitization training: Gradually increase the duration of your absences, starting with short periods and gradually extending the time. Reward your dog for calm behavior during your absences to help them feel more comfortable being alone.

Step 3: Provide interactive toys: Leave interactive toys or food puzzles to keep your dog mentally engaged while you're away. These toys can help distract them and reduce anxiety.

Step 4: Consider crate training: For some dogs, crate training can provide a sense of security and reduce anxiety when left alone. Ensure the crate is a positive and comfortable space for your dog, and gradually increase the duration of crate time.

> **Attention-Seeking Behaviors**

Dogs may engage in destructive behaviors as a way to get attention from their owners.

Step 1: Ignore unwanted behaviors: If your dog engages in attention-seeking behaviors like jumping, pawing, or barking for attention, ignore those behaviors. Avoid rewarding the behavior with attention, as it reinforces the behavior.

Step 2: Reinforce positive behaviors: Give attention and rewards when your dog displays desired behaviors, such as calmness or engaging with appropriate toys. This helps redirect their focus onto positive activities.

Step 3: Teach alternative behaviors: Teach your dog alternative behaviors to replace attention-seeking behaviors. For example, teach them to sit or lie down quietly to earn attention and rewards.

Step 4: Increase interactive play and training: Engage in regular interactive play sessions and training activities with your dog. This helps provide the attention and mental stimulation they crave in a positive and structured manner.

ENGAGING DOGS WITH COMPLEX PROBLEM-SOLVING TASKS

Engaging your dog in complex problem-solving tasks is a great way to provide mental stimulation and keep their minds active. These tasks can range from interactive puzzles to scavenger hunts that require your dog to use their problem-solving skills. Here's a step-by-step guide on how to engage your dog with complex problem-solving tasks, along with an example of exercises:

Step 1: Assess your dog's abilities and interests.

Take some time to understand your dog's strengths, weaknesses, and interests. Consider their breed, age, and previous training experience. This will help you select appropriate problem-solving tasks that will challenge and engage them.

Step 2: Start with simple tasks and gradually increase difficulty.

Introduce your dog to problem-solving tasks gradually, starting with simpler exercises and progressing to more complex ones. This allows your dog to build confidence and develop their problem-solving skills over time.

Step 3: Use positive reinforcement and rewards.

Positive reinforcement is crucial in training and engaging your dog. Use treats, praise, and rewards to motivate and reinforce their efforts during problem-solving tasks. This will encourage them to continue engaging and solving puzzles.

Step 4: Provide clear instructions and guidance.

When introducing a problem-solving task, provide clear instructions and guide your dog through the process. Break down the task into smaller steps, demonstrating and assisting them as needed. This will help your dog understand the objective and develop problem-solving strategies.

Step 5: Encourage independent thinking.

As your dog becomes more familiar with problem-solving tasks, encourage independent thinking and decision-making. Step back and allow them to explore different solutions. Avoid immediately providing the answer or intervening unless necessary.

Step 6: Offer support and assistance when needed.

While encouraging independent thinking, be attentive to your dog's progress. If they become stuck or frustrated, offer support and assistance. Provide gentle guidance or hints to help them find a solution, but allow them to make the final discovery themselves.

Step 7: Vary the problem-solving tasks.

To keep your dog engaged and prevent boredom, vary the problem-solving tasks you offer. Introduce different types of puzzles, challenges, or scavenger hunts. This will keep their minds sharp and provide a variety of mental stimulation.

Example of exercises:

➢ **The Cup Game**

The Cup Game involves using cups or containers to hide treats, requiring your dog to figure out which cup holds the reward.

Instructions:

✓ Place three cups upside down on the floor in a line.
✓ Let your dog watch as you place a treat under one of the cups.
✓ Shuffle the cups around quickly, mixing up their positions.
✓ Encourage your dog to use their paw or nose to indicate the cup with the treat.
✓ Reward your dog with the treat if they choose the correct cup.
✓ Gradually increase the difficulty by adding more cups or increasing the speed of the shuffle.

➤ **Doggy Sudoku**

Doggy Sudoku is a puzzle game that requires your dog to use their problem-solving skills to find the correct placement for treats or toys.

Instructions:

- ✓ Create a grid on a mat or piece of paper using treats or toys as placeholders.
- ✓ Show your dog one treat or toy and place it in the correct spot on the grid.
- ✓ Encourage your dog to find the correct placement for the remaining treats or toys.
- ✓ Reward your dog with praise and treats when they correctly place an item.
- ✓ Continue until all the items are correctly placed on the grid.

➤ **Treat Dispenser Puzzle**

A treat dispenser puzzle is a toy that requires your dog to manipulate it in various ways to access hidden treats.

Instructions:

- ✓ Provide your dog with a treat dispenser puzzle toy (e.g., a puzzle ball or cube).
- ✓ Fill the toy with your dog's favorite treats or kibble.
- ✓ Show your dog how the toy works by demonstrating how to roll, spin, or flip it to release the treats.
- ✓ Encourage your dog to interact with the toy and figure out how to access the treats.
- ✓ Reward your dog with praise and additional treats when they successfully retrieve the treats from the toy.

➤ **Canine Sniff and Search**

Canine Sniff and Search is an activity that taps into your dog's natural scenting abilities, requiring them to search for hidden treats or objects using their nose.

Instructions:

- ✓ Start with a few treats or toys and hide them in easy-to-find locations.

- ✓ Encourage your dog to use their nose to search for and find the hidden items.
- ✓ Provide verbal cues like "Find it" or "Search" to indicate the activity.
- ✓ Gradually increase the difficulty by hiding the items in more challenging spots or using scent cues to guide your dog.
- ✓ Reward your dog with praise and treats each time they successfully locate a hidden item.

➢ **Interactive Feeder Toy Challenge**

Interactive feeder toys are puzzle toys that require your dog to solve various mechanisms or puzzles to access their food.

Instructions:

- ✓ Provide your dog with an interactive feeder toy (e.g., a toy with compartments, sliders, or mazes).
- ✓ Fill the toy with your dog's regular kibble or treats.
- ✓ Demonstrate how to manipulate the toy to release the food.
- ✓ Encourage your dog to interact with the toy and figure out how to access their meal.
- ✓ Reward your dog with praise and additional treats when they successfully solve the puzzle and retrieve their food.

➢ **DIY Obstacle Course**

Create an indoor or outdoor obstacle course using household items to challenge your dog's problem-solving and physical abilities.

Instructions:

- ✓ Set up a course using items like chairs, tunnels, cones, ramps, or hula hoops.
- ✓ Guide your dog through the course, demonstrating how to navigate each obstacle.
- ✓ Use treats and praise to motivate your dog and reward them for successfully completing each obstacle.

- ✓ Gradually increase the difficulty by adding new challenges or obstacles to the course.
- ✓ Allow your dog to explore and find their own solutions to navigate the course.

➢ **Sequential Toy Play**

Sequential Toy Play involves presenting your dog with a series of toys or puzzles that they must solve in a specific order to access rewards.

Instructions:

- ✓ Gather a variety of toys or puzzles with different mechanisms (e.g., puzzle boxes, treat-dispensing toys, or interactive games).
- ✓ Present the toys to your dog one at a time, starting with the easiest one.
- ✓ Encourage your dog to interact with and solve each toy or puzzle to access the reward.
- ✓ Once they successfully solve one toy, move on to the next in a predetermined sequence.
- ✓ Reward your dog with praise and treats for completing each toy in the sequence.

STIMULATING COGNITIVE ABILITIES THROUGH INTERACTIVE GAMES

Here are few interactive games you can play with your dog:

Treat Hunt

This game engages your dog's sense of smell and provides mental stimulation.

Instructions:

- ✓ Start by having your dog sit and stay in one area of the house.
- ✓ While your dog is waiting, hide treats or toys in various locations around the house.
- ✓ Release your dog and encourage them to find the hidden treats by following their nose.
- ✓ Offer praise and rewards when they successfully locate the treats.

Obstacle Course

An obstacle course helps improve your dog's physical fitness, coordination, and obedience. Instructions:

- ✓ Set up a course in your yard or a designated area using items such as cones, hula hoops, tunnels, or low jumps.

- ✓ Guide your dog through the course, using treats and praise as rewards for completing each obstacle.

- ✓ Start with simple obstacles and gradually introduce more challenging ones as your dog becomes comfortable.

Kong Toy Challenge

This game keeps your dog mentally stimulated and rewards them with treats. Instructions:

- ✓ Fill a Kong toy with your dog's favorite treats or kibble.

- ✓ Give the Kong toy to your dog and encourage them to figure out how to get the treats out.

- ✓ You can freeze the Kong toy to make it more challenging and extend the playtime.

Find Your Toy

This game encourages your dog to use their sense of smell and memory. Instructions:

- ✓ Begin by having your dog sit and stay in one area.

- ✓ Show your dog one of their favorite toys and let them sniff and become familiar with it.

- ✓ Ask your dog to stay while you hide the toy in another room or behind an object.

- ✓ Release your dog and encourage them to find the toy by following their nose.

✓ Reward your dog with praise and playtime when they successfully locate their toy.

Scent Discrimination

This game challenges your dog's scenting abilities and helps develop their focus. Instructions:

✓ Place several containers, such as small boxes or cups, on the ground.

✓ Put a treat or an item with a strong scent in one of the containers.

✓ Encourage your dog to sniff and indicate the container with the scent.

✓ Reward your dog when they correctly identify the scented container.

Bobbing for Treats

This game provides a fun way for your dog to retrieve treats from a water-filled container. Instructions:

✓ Fill a shallow tub or a large bowl with water.

✓ Place floating treats or small toys in the water.

✓ Encourage your dog to reach into the water with their nose or paws to retrieve the treats.

✓ Praise and reward your dog when they successfully retrieve the treats.

Flirt Pole

The flirt pole is a great game for dogs with high prey drive, providing physical exercise and mental stimulation. Instructions:

✓ Attach a soft toy or a flirt pole toy to a long pole or string.

✓ Move the toy around in different patterns, encouraging your dog to chase and catch it.

✓ Allow your dog to catch and play with the toy, but always let them win occasionally.

DIY Snuffle Mat

A snuffle mat provides a fun and interactive way for your dog to search for treats. Instructions:

- ✓ Take a rubber mat or a piece of fabric and cut small holes or strips into it.

- ✓ Sprinkle treats or kibble into the holes or tuck them into the strips.

- ✓ Let your dog use their nose to search for and retrieve the treats from the mat.

Shell Game

This game tests your dog's memory and decision-making skills. Instructions:

- ✓ Line up three cups or containers in a row.

- ✓ Show your dog a treat and place it under one of the cups while they're watching.

- ✓ Shuffle the cups around quickly and encourage your dog to find the treat by indicating the correct cup.

- ✓ Reward your dog when they choose the correct cup.

Soccer

Playing soccer with your dog can be a fun way to engage them physically and mentally. Instructions:

- ✓ Use a dog-friendly soccer ball or a soft toy that your dog can push with their nose.

- ✓ Encourage your dog to push the ball with their nose or paws.

- ✓ Use positive reinforcement and rewards to motivate and praise your dog as they interact with the ball.

Name That Toy

This game helps your dog learn the names of their toys and enhances their cognitive skills. Instructions:

- ✓ Gather a few of your dog's toys and give each one a distinct name.

- ✓ Place the toys in a line or spread them out on the floor.

- ✓ Say the name of one toy and encourage your dog to fetch that specific toy.

- ✓ Reward your dog with praise and treats when they bring back the correct toy.

Musical Chairs

A canine version of the classic game, Musical Chairs adds excitement and mental stimulation for your dog. Instructions:

- ✓ Arrange a circle of chairs or mats on the floor.

- ✓ While playing music, walk your dog around the chairs in a clockwise direction.

- ✓ When the music stops, command your dog to sit on one of the chairs or mats.

- ✓ If your dog sits on the correct spot, reward them with a treat or praise. Remove one chair or mat after each round and repeat the game.

Water Splash

This game helps your dog cool down during hot weather and provides a fun sensory experience. Instructions:

- ✓ Fill a small kiddie pool or a shallow container with water.

- ✓ Encourage your dog to splash and play in the water.

- ✓ You can also place floating toys or treats in the water to make it more enticing for your dog.

- ✓ Monitor your dog to ensure their safety and prevent excessive drinking of pool water.

Balloon Volleyball

Balloon volleyball is a gentle and entertaining game that improves your dog's coordination and focus. Instructions:

- ✓ Blow up a balloon and keep it from touching the ground.

- ✓ Encourage your dog to hit the balloon with their paws or nose, keeping it in the air.

- ✓ Applaud and reward your dog for successful hits and attempts to keep the balloon aloft.

- ✓ Ensure the balloon is large enough to prevent accidental ingestion.

Copycat

This game strengthens the bond between you and your dog while encouraging them to mimic your actions. Instructions:

- ✓ Choose a space with room for movement.

- ✓ Start by performing simple movements, such as jumping, spinning, or crawling.

- ✓ Encourage your dog to imitate your actions by using verbal cues or hand signals.

- ✓ Reward your dog with treats and praise when they successfully mimic your movements.

PART 5

TAILORED

MENTAL EXERCISES

FOR DIFFERENT NEEDS

Chapter 1:

Mental Stimulation for Puppies

and Young Dogs

AGE-APPROPRIATE EXERCISES AND DEVELOPMENTAL STAGES

1. **Infants (up to 6 months)**

   a. Tummy time:

   - ✓ Lay a soft blanket or mat on the floor.
   - ✓ Gently place the puppy on its tummy, supporting its weight.
   - ✓ Encourage the puppy to lift its head and explore its surroundings.
   - ✓ Start with short sessions of 2-3 minutes and gradually increase the duration as the puppy gets comfortable.

   b. Crawling practice:

   - ✓ Set up a safe area with cushions, low obstacles, and tunnels.
   - ✓ Place the puppy at one end and encourage it to crawl through the obstacles.
   - ✓ Use toys or treats to motivate the puppy to explore and navigate the space.
   - ✓ Supervise the puppy to ensure safety and provide guidance if needed.

   c. Gentle object exploration:

   - ✓ Introduce a variety of puppy-safe toys with different textures, shapes, and sizes.
   - ✓ Allow the puppy to explore the toys at its own pace.
   - ✓ Rotate the toys to maintain novelty and prevent boredom.
   - ✓ Always monitor the puppy during playtime to ensure safety.

2. Puppies (6 months to 1 year)

a. Short walks:

- ✓ Attach a lightweight leash to the puppy's collar or harness.
- ✓ Start with short walks in a quiet, familiar environment.
- ✓ Walk at a relaxed pace, allowing the puppy to sniff and explore within boundaries.
- ✓ Gradually increase the duration and distance of the walks as the puppy's endurance improves.

b. Basic obedience training:

- ✓ Teach simple commands like sit, stay, and come.
- ✓ Use positive reinforcement techniques such as treats and praise.
- ✓ Break down each command into small steps and reward the puppy for successful attempts.
- ✓ Practice the commands in a distraction-free environment initially and gradually add more distractions.

c. Interactive play:

- ✓ Engage in games like fetch or hide-and-seek to improve coordination and strengthen the bond.
- ✓ Use a soft, lightweight ball or toy for fetch.
- ✓ Hide treats or toys in various locations and encourage the puppy to search and find them.
- ✓ Rotate the games to keep them engaging and exciting for the puppy.

➢ Adolescents (1 to 2 years)

a. Long walks or jogs:

- ✓ Increase the duration and intensity of walks or include short jogging sessions.
- ✓ Ensure the puppy is properly warmed up before jogging to prevent injuries.
- ✓ Vary the route and introduce new environments to keep the walks interesting.

✓ Consider using a harness for added control and comfort.

b. Advanced obedience training:

✓ Teach more complex commands such as "down," "leave it," or "heel."

✓ Focus on improving the puppy's responsiveness and reliability.

✓ Gradually increase the distractions during training sessions to generalize the commands.

c. Agility training:

✓ Set up a small agility course in the backyard or a safe open area.

✓ Introduce obstacles such as tunnels, jumps, and weave poles.

✓ Use treats and positive reinforcement to guide the puppy through the course.

✓ Start with low heights and gradually increase the difficulty level as the puppy gains confidence.

SOCIALIZATION AND MENTAL STIMULATION FOR WELL-ROUNDED DOGS

A well-rounded dog is not only physically healthy but also mentally and emotionally balanced. It is important for dog owners to provide proper exercise, mental stimulation, and socialization opportunities to ensure their dogs develop into well-rounded companions.

Dog parks or playdates:

✓ Find a local dog park or arrange playdates with other well-behaved and vaccinated dogs.

✓ Ensure the environment is safe and secure for off-leash play.

✓ Introduce your dog to other dogs gradually, starting with calm and friendly interactions.

✓ Observe their body language and intervene if any signs of discomfort or aggression arise.

✓ Encourage positive interactions and play while monitoring their behavior.

Group training classes:

✓ Research and enroll your dog in a reputable group training class.

✓ Choose a class that emphasizes positive reinforcement techniques.

✓ Attend regular sessions to expose your dog to new people and dogs in a controlled environment.

✓ Practice obedience commands and engage in group activities.

✓ Gradually increase the difficulty level of exercises to challenge your dog's social skills.

Controlled exposure to new environments:

✓ Take your dog on regular outings to different environments, such as parks, busy streets, or cafes.

✓ Start with quieter and less overwhelming locations and gradually progress to busier places.

✓ Allow your dog to observe and interact with various sights, sounds, and smells.

✓ Reward calm and confident behavior with treats and praise.

✓ Provide a safe space, such as a mat or blanket, where your dog can retreat if feeling overwhelmed.

MENTAL EXERCISES FOR ENERGETIC PUPPIES

There are dogs that possess high levels of energy and enthusiasm. They are often characterized by their playful and active nature, frequently engaging in various physical activities and requiring ample mental stimulation. These puppies thrive on regular exercise, mental challenges, and engaging playtime to help them expend their energy in positive ways and maintain a healthy balance of physical and mental stimulation. It's important to provide them with appropriate outlets for their energy to ensure their overall well-being and to prevent boredom-related behaviors.

Memory Game:

✓ Line up a few cups or bowls in a row.

- ✓ Show your puppy a treat and place it under one of the cups.
- ✓ Allow your puppy to watch as you shuffle the cups.
- ✓ Wait a few seconds, then encourage your puppy to indicate which cup has the treat.
- ✓ Reward your puppy when they choose the correct cup, and repeat the game with different cup arrangements.
- ✓ Tug-and-Freeze:
- ✓ Freeze a damp cloth or rope toy in a plastic bag.
- ✓ Give the frozen toy to your puppy and engage in a gentle game of tug-of-war.
- ✓ The coolness of the toy provides soothing relief for teething puppies while offering mental and physical stimulation.
- ✓ Monitor your puppy to ensure they don't chew on or swallow the frozen toy.

Bubble Chasing:

- ✓ Use a pet-safe bubble solution and bubble wand.
- ✓ Blow bubbles in an open area and encourage your puppy to chase and pop them.
- ✓ This game provides mental and physical exercise while adding an element of fun and novelty.

Stairway Dash:

- ✓ Find a safe and carpeted staircase.
- ✓ Stand at the bottom of the stairs and call your puppy's name or use a toy to entice them.
- ✓ Encourage your puppy to race up the stairs to reach you.
- ✓ Praise and reward your puppy when they reach the top of the stairs.
- ✓ Make sure the stairs are not too steep or slippery, and supervise your puppy during the game.

Find the Hidden Sock:

- ✓ Take a clean sock and let your puppy smell it.
- ✓ Ask your puppy to sit and stay in one room while you hide the sock in another room.

- ✓ Release your puppy and encourage them to find the hidden sock using their nose.
- ✓ When your puppy successfully locates the sock, reward them with praise and a treat.

Balloon Bounce:

- ✓ Blow up a balloon and let your puppy see and hear it.
- ✓ Toss the balloon gently in the air and encourage your puppy to jump and paw at it.
- ✓ Supervise your puppy during this game to ensure they don't puncture the balloon.
- ✓ The bouncing balloon provides visual and physical stimulation for your puppy.

Synchronized Fetch:

- ➢ Play fetch with two identical toys or balls.

- ✓ Start by throwing one toy and encouraging your puppy to fetch it.
- ✓ As your puppy returns with the first toy, throw the second toy in the opposite direction.
- ✓ Your puppy will experience the challenge of deciding which toy to retrieve and will engage in active play.

Simon Says:

- ✓ Use basic obedience commands such as sit, lie down, stay, and come.
- ✓ Start with a command such as "sit" and reward your puppy when they comply.
- ✓ Gradually introduce the game element by saying "Simon says sit" and rewarding your puppy only when they sit after hearing "Simon says."
- ✓ This game challenges your puppy's listening skills and reinforces obedience commands.

Chase the Laser Pointer:

- ✓ Use a laser pointer and direct the laser beam on the floor or against a wall.
- ✓ Move the laser pointer around, creating quick movements and changing directions.
- ✓ Encourage your puppy to chase and try to "catch" the moving laser dot.
- ✓ Make sure to never shine the laser pointer directly into your puppy's eyes.

Stuffed Kong Challenge:

✓ Take a Kong toy or any treat-dispensing toy with a hollow center.

✓ Fill the toy with a mixture of wet and dry dog food, or peanut butter and treats.

✓ Freeze the stuffed toy overnight or until the filling is solid.

✓ Give the frozen Kong to your puppy, and they'll have to work to get the treats out as it gradually thaws.

Digging Pit:

✓ Create a designated digging area in your yard or use a sandbox filled with sand or soil.

✓ Bury some treats or toys just below the surface of the digging pit.

✓ Encourage your puppy to dig and search for the hidden treasures.

✓ This game allows your puppy to satisfy their natural digging instincts in a controlled and appropriate manner.

Name That Smell:

✓ Gather different scented items like essential oils or spices.

✓ Present each item to your puppy and let them sniff it.

✓ Assign a specific command or action to each scent, such as sitting or touching their nose to your hand.

✓ Test your puppy's ability to associate each scent with the correct command and reward them for their responses.

Chapter 2:

Mental Stimulation for Adult and Senior Dogs

ADJUSTING EXERCISES TO ACCOMMODATE ENERGY LEVELS

It's important to tailor physical activities to suit your adult and seniors dog's energy levels and provide appropriate exercise without overexerting them. Here are some strategies to help you adjust exercises for them:

➢ **Consult with Your Veterinarian**

  ✓ Before making any changes to your dog's exercise routine, consult with your veterinarian. They can assess your dog's overall health, energy levels, and any specific considerations based on their age or medical conditions.

➢ **Understand Your Dog's Energy Level**

  ✓ Observe and understand your dog's energy level and behavior patterns. Some dogs are naturally high-energy, while others may have lower energy levels. Adapt exercises to match their individual needs.

➢ **Adjust Exercise Duration and Intensity**

  ✓ Shorten the duration of exercise sessions for senior dogs compared to adult dogs. Gradually increase or decrease exercise time based on your dog's energy levels and any signs of fatigue or discomfort.
  ✓ Consider lower-impact exercises, such as gentle walks or swimming, for senior dogs. Avoid high-impact activities that may strain their joints or muscles.

➤ **Provide Mental Stimulation**

   ✓ Engage your dog's mind through interactive games, puzzle toys, and obedience training. Mental stimulation is just as important as physical exercise and helps tire out your dog mentally.

   ✓ Incorporate training sessions that focus on mental exercises and problem-solving. Teach new tricks or work on reinforcing obedience commands.

➤ **Consider the Environment**

   ✓ Take the weather and temperature into account. Adjust exercise times to avoid extreme heat or cold, which can impact your dog's energy levels and overall comfort.

   ✓ Provide a comfortable and safe environment for exercise. Clear any obstacles or hazards that may pose a risk to your dog's well-being.

➤ **Frequent Potty Breaks**

   ✓ Senior dogs may have reduced bladder control and may need more frequent potty breaks. Plan exercise sessions accordingly, allowing for breaks to give them an opportunity to relieve themselves.

➤ **Monitor Your Dog's Response**

   ✓ Pay attention to your dog's body language and behavior during and after exercise. Watch for signs of fatigue, excessive panting, lameness, or any discomfort.

   ✓ If you notice any adverse reactions or if your dog seems excessively tired or reluctant to exercise, consult with your veterinarian to ensure their health and well-being.

➤ **Incorporate Rest and Recovery**

   ✓ Ensure your dog has ample time to rest and recover between exercise sessions, especially for senior dogs who may require longer recovery periods.

✓ Provide a comfortable and quiet space where your dog can relax and unwind after exercise.

MAINTAINING COGNITIVE HEALTH IN AGING DOGS

To ensure the overall well-being and quality of life for aging dogs, it is crucial to maintain their cognitive health. Here are some tips and strategies to help keep your senior dog mentally sharp:

➤ Prioritize Mental Stimulation: Engage your senior dog's mind through regular mental exercises and enrichment activities. This can include interactive toys, puzzle games, scent work, and training sessions.

➤ Create a Stimulating Environment: Provide a variety of toys, objects, and puzzles to keep your senior dog mentally engaged. Rotate and introduce new items regularly to prevent boredom.

➤ Regular Exercise: Incorporate age-appropriate physical exercise into your senior dog's routine. Physical activity supports brain health and mental well-being.

➤ Optimize their Diet: Feed your senior dog a balanced diet that includes brain-supporting nutrients such as antioxidants and omega-3 fatty acids. Consult with your veterinarian for specific dietary recommendations.

➤ Consider Supplements: Discuss with your veterinarian the possibility of adding cognitive-supporting supplements to your senior dog's diet, such as omega-3 fatty acids or specialized formulas.

➤ Promote Social Interaction: Ensure your senior dog has regular social interaction with you, other pets, or friendly humans. This helps stimulate their cognitive abilities and prevents social isolation.

➤ Establish a Consistent Routine: Maintain a predictable daily routine and a familiar environment to reduce anxiety and confusion. Consistency provides cognitive stability.

- ➢ Regular Veterinary Check-ups: Schedule routine check-ups with your veterinarian to monitor your senior dog's cognitive function and overall health. They can provide guidance and detect any potential cognitive decline.

- ➢ Adapt Training Sessions: Continue training activities with your senior dog, adjusting them to their abilities and physical limitations. Reinforce previous commands and gradually introduce new ones.

- ➢ Shower Them with Love and Attention: Give your senior dog plenty of love, attention, and affection. Positive interactions and a nurturing environment contribute to their overall well-being and cognitive health.

ADAPTING MENTAL EXERCISES FOR SENIOR DOGS' ABILITIES

To make sure senior dogs can comfortably participate in and benefit from mental exercises, it's crucial to adapt the activities to their abilities. This will help keep their minds active and engaged while considering any limitations they may have. By making a few adjustments, you can create an enjoyable and beneficial experience for your senior dog.

- ✓ Puzzle Toys: Choose puzzle toys that are suitable for senior dogs with limited mobility or dental issues. Opt for softer textures and easier difficulty levels to accommodate their needs.

- ✓ Scent Work: Engage senior dogs in scent work activities, where they use their sense of smell to find hidden treats or scented objects. This taps into their natural abilities and provides mental stimulation.

- ✓ Basic Obedience Refreshers: Continue to practice basic obedience commands with senior dogs to keep their minds active. Use positive reinforcement techniques and be patient and understanding of any limitations they may have.

- ✓ Brain Games: Incorporate brain games that focus on memory and problem-solving skills. For example, play memory games by placing a few cups upside down and hiding a treat under one of them. Your dog has to remember which cup has the treat.

✓ Nose Work: Engage senior dogs in nose work activities that involve searching for specific scents or tracking scents in a controlled environment. This taps into their natural abilities and provides mental and sensory stimulation.

Here are examples of adapted mental exercises for a senior dog:

Sniff and Find Treats

Step-by-step guide:

➢ Choose a quiet and comfortable area in your home for the exercise. Make sure it's free from distractions.

➢ Gather some soft, high-value treats that are easy for your senior dog to chew. Ensure they are small enough for your dog to consume without any difficulty.

➢ Start by sitting with your senior dog and showing them one treat in your hand.

➢ Encourage your dog to sniff the treat by bringing it close to their nose. Give them verbal cues like "sniff" or "find it" to help them understand the objective.

➢ Once your dog has shown interest in the treat, gently toss it a short distance away. Make sure it's within their reach and not too far to cause strain.

➢ Allow your dog to follow their nose and find the treat. Offer positive verbal reinforcement, such as saying "good job" or "well done," when they locate and consume the treat.

➢ Repeat this process with additional treats, gradually increasing the difficulty by tossing them slightly farther away or in different directions.

➢ Observe your senior dog's energy levels and physical comfort throughout the exercise. Take breaks as needed and adjust the distance or intensity of the activity to suit their abilities.

- You can also introduce scent cues by rubbing a treat against a specific object, such as a toy or cloth, before hiding it. This adds an extra mental challenge for your dog to follow the scent and find the hidden treat.

- End the exercise on a positive note with verbal praise and a final treat reward.

Gentle Nose Work

Step-by-step guide:

- Choose a quiet and familiar area in your home where you can conduct the exercise. Make sure there are no hazards or obstacles that could cause any harm to your senior dog.

- Gather a few small, soft treats that are easy for your dog to consume. You can also use scent-infused treats or treats with a strong aroma to make it easier for your senior dog to locate them.

- Start by having your senior dog sit or lie down comfortably in front of you.

- Hold a treat in your hand and present it to your dog's nose, allowing them to sniff it and become interested.

- Slowly move your hand with the treat in front of your dog's nose in a gentle sweeping motion, guiding them to follow the scent trail with their nose.

- Gradually increase the difficulty by hiding the treat in a nearby location within the room. Start with easy hiding spots, such as behind a cushion or under a lightweight object.

- Encourage your senior dog to use their sense of smell to locate the hidden treat. Offer verbal cues like "find it" or "search" to guide them.

- Celebrate and praise your dog when they successfully find the treat. You can also provide additional treats as rewards for their effort.

➤ Repeat the process, gradually increasing the difficulty of the hiding spots. You can hide treats in different rooms or elevate the challenge by placing them slightly higher off the ground.

➤ If your senior dog has mobility issues, you can modify the exercise by using scent boxes or containers. Place the treat inside a container with holes or an open lid, allowing your dog to use their nose to discover the treat.

➤ Always monitor your dog's energy levels and physical comfort throughout the exercise. Adjust the difficulty and duration as needed to ensure it remains enjoyable and manageable for them.

Food Puzzle Fun

Step-by-step guide:

➤ Choose a food puzzle toy suitable for your senior dog's size and abilities. There are various options available, such as treat balls, puzzle feeders, or interactive mats.

➤ Select a soft, high-value treat or a portion of your dog's regular food that they enjoy. Ensure the treats are small and easy to handle.

➤ Introduce the food puzzle toy to your senior dog, allowing them to sniff and investigate it. Encourage their interest by placing a few treats on top or inside the toy.

➤ Show your dog how the food puzzle works. If it's a treat ball, demonstrate rolling it to release treats. If it's a puzzle feeder, show them how to manipulate the different components to access the food.

➤ Let your senior dog try the food puzzle on their own. Observe and offer gentle guidance if needed, helping them understand how to solve the puzzle and access the treats inside.

➤ If your dog seems to struggle with the food puzzle or gets frustrated, offer assistance by providing additional verbal cues or physically demonstrating the steps again.

- Once your dog successfully obtains the treats from the food puzzle, provide verbal praise and encouragement. You can also offer extra treats as rewards.

- Vary the food puzzles you use to keep the activity engaging and mentally stimulating for your senior dog. Experiment with different designs, textures, and levels of difficulty to challenge them.

- Observe your senior dog's energy levels and physical comfort during the activity. Adjust the difficulty level or duration of the session to suit their abilities and prevent fatigue.

- Clean the food puzzle toy thoroughly after each use to maintain hygiene and ensure it remains enticing for your senior dog.

Gentle Training and Trick Practice

Step-by-step guide:

- Choose a quiet and comfortable area in your home where you can conduct the exercise without distractions.

- Select a few simple commands or tricks that your senior dog already knows well. Examples can include "sit," "stay," "shake paws," or "spin."

- Start by refreshing your senior dog's memory of the chosen commands or tricks. Use gentle verbal cues and hand signals that they are familiar with.

- Practice each command or trick individually, giving your senior dog ample time to respond. Be patient and offer gentle guidance as needed.

- Use high-value treats or soft rewards to motivate your senior dog during the training session. Ensure the treats are small and easy for them to consume.

- Keep the training sessions short and enjoyable. Older dogs may tire more quickly, so it's important to maintain their engagement without overwhelming them.

➢ Gradually introduce new commands or tricks to provide mental stimulation. Choose ones that are within your senior dog's physical capabilities and won't put excessive strain on their joints.

➢ Adapt the difficulty level of the exercises as needed. If your senior dog struggles with a particular command or trick, simplify it or break it down into smaller steps.

➢ Offer plenty of positive reinforcement, praise, and rewards when your senior dog successfully follows a command or performs a trick. This will help maintain their motivation and enthusiasm.

➢ End the training session on a positive note, with a final reward and some gentle petting or cuddling to show your appreciation.

➢ Repeat the training exercises regularly to reinforce your senior dog's existing skills and introduce new challenges gradually.

PART 6

REAL-LIFE

SUCCESS STORIES

AND RESOURCES

Chapter 1:

Inspiring Dog-Owner Relationships through Mental Exercises

CASE STUDIES OF DOGS' BEHAVIORAL TRANSFORMATIONS

This section presents case studies highlighting the remarkable transformations observed in dogs through proper training, rehabilitation, and behavior modification techniques. These real-life examples demonstrate the potential for positive change and offer insights into effective approaches for dealing with behavioral challenges in dogs.

Case Study 1: Overcoming Aggression

In this case, a dog named Max displayed aggressive behavior towards other dogs, which made it challenging for his owner to take him on walks or socialize with other pets. With the guidance of a professional dog trainer, a comprehensive behavior modification plan was implemented, including desensitization and counter-conditioning techniques. Over time, Max's aggression diminished, and he learned alternative behaviors, enabling him to interact peacefully with other dogs.

Case Study 2: Separation Anxiety Management

Lola, a rescue dog, suffered from severe separation anxiety, leading to destructive behavior whenever her owner left the house. To address this issue, a gradual desensitization program was implemented, gradually exposing Lola to short periods of alone time. Additionally, mental stimulation techniques, such as food puzzles and interactive toys, were used to keep Lola engaged and mentally occupied. Through consistent training and patient efforts, Lola's separation anxiety significantly improved, allowing her owner to leave the house without causing distress.

Case Study 3: Fear and Noise Phobia

Bella, a Labrador Retriever, had an extreme fear of loud noises, especially thunderstorms and fireworks. This fear would lead to panic attacks and destructive behavior. A behavior modification program was designed, which involved gradual exposure to recorded sounds of thunderstorms, coupled with positive reinforcement. Over time, Bella's fear response reduced, and she became more resilient to loud noises, enabling her to remain calm during such situations.

Case Study 4: Overcoming Leash Reactivity

Sam, a high-energy dog, exhibited intense reactivity on the leash, lunging and barking at other dogs during walks. A positive reinforcement-based training program was implemented, focusing on teaching Sam alternative behaviors and providing rewards for calm responses. With consistent training and patience, Sam's leash reactivity gradually diminished, allowing for more enjoyable walks and improved social interactions.

TESTIMONIALS FROM DOG OWNERS ON THE POWER OF MENTAL STIMULATION

Here are some testimonials from dog owners who have witnessed the transformative power of mental stimulation on their pets' lives. These firsthand accounts demonstrate the positive impact mental enrichment activities can have on dogs, fostering their cognitive abilities and promoting a happier, healthier lifestyle.

> **Sophie - Labrador Retriever Owner**

"Introducing mental stimulation activities to my Labrador Retriever, Bella, has been a game-changer. She used to get restless and exhibit destructive behaviors, but now, she's engaged, focused, and much calmer. Puzzle toys and training games have transformed her behavior for the better!"

➤ **Mike - Border Collie Owner**

"I can't emphasize enough how much mental stimulation has impacted my Border Collie, Max. He's a highly intelligent breed, and without mental challenges, he would become bored and restless. With interactive toys and scent work, Max is not only entertained, but his obedience and focus have skyrocketed."

➤ **Emma - Shih Tzu Owner**

"Even though Shih Tzus are known for their small size, they have big personalities. Mental stimulation has become an essential part of my Shih Tzu's routine. Puzzle toys have improved his problem-solving skills, and it's incredible to see how engaged and content he is after each play session."

➤ **Mark - German Shepherd Owner**

"German Shepherds are intelligent and energetic dogs, and mental stimulation is vital for their well-being. Incorporating training games and interactive activities has helped channel my German Shepherd's energy in a positive way. He's more focused, responsive, and our bond has grown stronger."

➤ **Sarah - Beagle Owner**

"Beagles have a keen sense of smell, and mental stimulation has tapped into that natural instinct for my dog, Cooper. Scent work and nose games have been a lifesaver. Cooper is now more mentally satisfied, and his behavior has improved. Mental stimulation has turned our walks into exciting adventures!"

➤ **David - Mixed Breed Owner**

"I adopted a mixed breed dog, Buddy, and he struggled with anxiety and restlessness. Mental stimulation activities like puzzle toys and agility training have transformed Buddy's behavior. He's more relaxed, and the mental challenges have given him a sense of purpose and confidence."

- **Jessica - Golden Retriever Owner**

"As a Golden Retriever owner, I've witnessed the power of mental stimulation in my dog, Charlie. Through obedience training, puzzle toys, and brain games, Charlie's focus and obedience have improved significantly. Mental stimulation has brought out the best in him and made him a happier, well-rounded dog."

Chapter 2:

Additional Resources and Further Reading

Recommended Books:

➤ "The Other End of the Leash: Why We Do What We Do Around Dogs" by Patricia McConnell

➤ "Inside of a Dog: What Dogs See, Smell, and Know" by Alexandra Horowitz

➤ "Don't Shoot the Dog!: The New Art of Teaching and Training" by Karen Pryor

➤ "The Power of Positive Dog Training" by Pat Miller

Websites and Online Communities:

➤ The Association of Professional Dog Trainers (APDT) - www.apdt.com

➤ Karen Pryor Academy - www.karenpryoracademy.com

➤ The Whole Dog Journal - www.whole-dog-journal.com

➤ Dog Training Reddit - www.reddit.com/r/Dogtraining

➤ The Online Dog Trainer - www.theonlinedogtrainer.com

Professional Training Programs and Workshops:

➤ Certification Council for Professional Dog Trainers (CCPDT) - www.ccpdt.org

➤ International Association of Animal Behavior Consultants (IAABC) - www.iaabc.org

➤ Academy for Dog Trainers - www.academyfordogtrainers.com

➤ Dog Trainer Professional - www.dogtrainerprofessional.com

➤ Karen Pryor Academy - www.karenpryoracademy.com

Further Reading on Canine Behavior and Mental Stimulation:

➤ "Decoding Your Dog: Explaining Common Dog Behaviors and How to Change Them" edited by American College of Veterinary Behaviorists

➤ "Dog Sense: How the New Science of Dog Behavior Can Make You a Better Friend to Your Pet" by John Bradshaw

➤ "Brain Games for Dogs: Fun Ways to Build a Strong Bond with Your Dog and Provide Mental Stimulation" by Claire Arrowsmith

➤ "The Dog's Mind: Understanding Your Dog's Behavior" by Bruce Fogle

CONCLUSION

AND FINAL THOUGHTS

Chapter 1:

Maintaining a Lifelong Commitment to Mental Stimulation

Recap of Key Takeaways and Lessons Learned

Throughout this journey of exploring the power of mental stimulation for dogs, there are several key takeaways and lessons learned that can help in maintaining a lifelong commitment to providing mental enrichment for your furry companion:

➤ Mental Stimulation is Vital: Understand that mental stimulation is not just a luxury but a necessity for dogs. It helps prevent boredom, reduces destructive behaviors, and promotes overall well-being.

➤ Variety is Key: Dogs thrive on novelty and new experiences. Incorporate a variety of mental stimulation activities such as puzzle toys, training games, scent work, and interactive play to keep them engaged and challenged.

➤ Tailor Activities to Your Dog's Breed and Personality: Different breeds have varying needs and preferences when it comes to mental stimulation. Take into consideration your dog's breed characteristics and individual personality traits to choose activities that align with their natural instincts and interests.

➤ Consistency and Routine: Establish a regular mental stimulation routine to provide your dog with predictable and structured activities. Consistency helps dogs develop a sense of security and stability.

Creating a Sustainable Mental Stimulation Routine

To maintain a lifelong commitment to mental stimulation, it is important to create a sustainable routine that fits into your lifestyle:

➢ Set Realistic Goals: Start with realistic goals and gradually increase the complexity and duration of mental stimulation activities. Don't overwhelm yourself or your dog with too much too soon.

➢ Schedule Dedicated Time: Dedicate specific times each day for mental stimulation activities. Consistency is key, so choose a schedule that works for you and stick to it.

➢ Incorporate Mental Challenges into Daily Life: Look for opportunities to incorporate mental challenges into your dog's daily routine. For example, you can use interactive feeding toys or scatter treats around the house to encourage problem-solving and foraging behaviors.

➢ Adapt as Your Dog Grows: As your dog matures and gains experience, adjust the level of difficulty and introduce new activities to keep them engaged and mentally stimulated.

Embracing the Journey of Continuous Learning and Growth

Mental stimulation is an ongoing process that requires continuous learning and adaptation:

➢ Stay Informed: Stay updated on the latest research, training techniques, and ideas for mental stimulation. Attend workshops, seminars, or join online communities to connect with fellow dog owners and professionals.

➢ Observe and Listen to Your Dog: Pay attention to your dog's cues and preferences. Observe their reactions and adjust the activities accordingly. Each dog is unique, and understanding their individual needs is crucial.

➢ Seek Professional Guidance: Consider working with a certified dog trainer or behaviorist to further enhance your understanding of mental stimulation and receive guidance tailored to your dog's specific needs.

➢ Enjoy the Journey: Embrace the process of continuous learning and growth alongside your dog. Enjoy the moments of discovery, the bond you build, and the joy of seeing your dog thrive through mental stimulation.

Chapter 2:

Your Success with Mental Exercises for

Dogs

To all fellow dog owners out there, I want to offer you encouragement and support as you continue your journey of exploring and expanding mental exercises for your beloved companions. The successes and milestones you achieve along the way are worth celebrating, and the bond you form with your dog through these activities is truly special.

As you engage in mental exercises with your dog, remember to celebrate every achievement, no matter how small. Whether it's solving a puzzle toy, learning a new trick, or demonstrating improved focus and obedience, each step forward is a testament to your dedication and your dog's growth. Take a moment to relish in the joy and pride you both feel when you accomplish these milestones together.

Sharing your experience and insights with others is invaluable. By connecting with fellow dog owners, you can exchange stories, ideas, and strategies, creating a supportive community that fosters growth and learning. Your unique experiences can inspire and motivate others to embark on their own journeys of mental stimulation. So, don't hesitate to share your successes, challenges, and the positive impact mental exercises have had on your dog's well-being.

Remember, the world of canine mental stimulation is vast and ever-evolving. As you continue on this path, keep exploring and expanding your repertoire of activities. Be open to trying new exercises, techniques, and games that resonate with your dog's personality, breed, and interests. Embrace the opportunity to learn from other dog owners and professionals who specialize in mental stimulation. Their insights and expertise can provide valuable guidance and inspire you to discover even more enriching experiences for your furry friend.

In your pursuit of mental exercises, don't forget to enjoy the journey. Embrace the moments of connection, growth, and discovery with your dog. Cherish the shared experiences, the wagging tails, and the sparkle in their eyes as they engage in stimulating activities. Together, you and your dog are embarking on a lifelong adventure of continuous learning and growth.

So, keep going, fellow dog owners! Your commitment to providing mental stimulation for your dogs is commendable, and the benefits you will witness in their behavior, focus, and overall well-being are immeasurable. Embrace the joy of this shared journey, and may your exploration of mental exercises bring you and your furry companion closer than ever before.

BONUS #1: DAILY MENTAL STIMULATION PLANNER

This Daily Mental Stimulation Planner is designed to help you create a structured routine and track your dog's progress in their mental stimulation journey. The planner includes dedicated sections for recording the type of exercise or activity you plan to engage your dog in. Whether it's puzzle toys, obedience training, scent work, or interactive games, you can clearly outline and organize each exercise.

The planner includes dedicated sections for recording the type of exercise or activity you plan to engage your dog in. Whether it's puzzle toys, obedience training, scent work, or interactive games, you can clearly outline and organize each exercise.

Date	Exercise	Duration	Level	Notes

Date	Exercise	Duration	Level	Notes

BONUS #2: TRACKING PROGRESS AND BEHAVIORAL CHANGES WORKSHEET

In this Tracking Progress and Behavioral Changes Worksheet, you will find a printable resource that empowers you to monitor your dog's behavior and track the improvements that arise from the implementation of mental exercises. This resource enables you to keep a record of your dog's behaviors, make observations, and assess any positive changes that occur over time. By utilizing this worksheet, you can actively monitor and measure the effectiveness of the mental exercises in improving your dog's behavior.

Behavior/Challenge	Exercise Implemented	Changes Observed

Behavior/Challenge	Exercise Implemented	Changes Observed

Behavior/Challenge	Exercise Implemented	Changes Observed

BONUS #3: CHECKLIST OF ESSENTIAL SUPPLIES FOR MENTAL EXERCISES

This appendix provides you with a checklist of essential supplies and materials needed for various mental exercises discussed in the book. The checklist will help you ensure that you have all the necessary supplies before you begin implementing the exercises, making it convenient and easy for you to prepare for each activity

➢ Interactive Toys:
- ☐ Puzzle toys
- ☐ Interactive feeding toys
- ☐ Tug toys
- ☐ Squeaky toys
- ☐ Interactive electronic toys

➢ Puzzle Games:
- ☐ Interactive puzzle games
- ☐ Brain teaser puzzles
- ☐ Labyrinth or maze games

➢ Scent Detection Tools:
- ☐ Scented training aids
- ☐ Scent detection kits
- ☐ Treat or toy containers with hidden scents

➢ Treat Dispensers:
- ☐ Treat balls or dispensers
- ☐ Snuffle mats
- ☐ Kong toys or similar treat-dispensing toys

➢ Agility Course Equipment:
- ☐ Agility tunnels
- ☐ Jumping hurdles or bars
- ☐ Weave poles
- ☐ Pause table or platform
- ☐ A-frame or dog walk ramps

- ➤ Other Supplies:
  - ☐ Clicker
  - ☐ Target stick or target mat
  - ☐ High-value treats
  - ☐ Treat pouch or container for storing treats
  - ☐ Timer or stopwatch
  - ☐ Notebook or journal
  - ☐ Pen or pencil
  - ☐ Training mat or non-slip surface
  - ☐ Training Leash or Harness
  - ☐ Cleaning Supplies

Made in the USA
Las Vegas, NV
29 December 2023

83695251R00072